DATE DUE

BIG S D 1 - 29 '80	
BIG S D 1 1 2 '81	
BIG S D 9 5 '84	
BIG S D 1 7 '86	
GREN 4 23 '86	
Mrs. O'B 3/96	

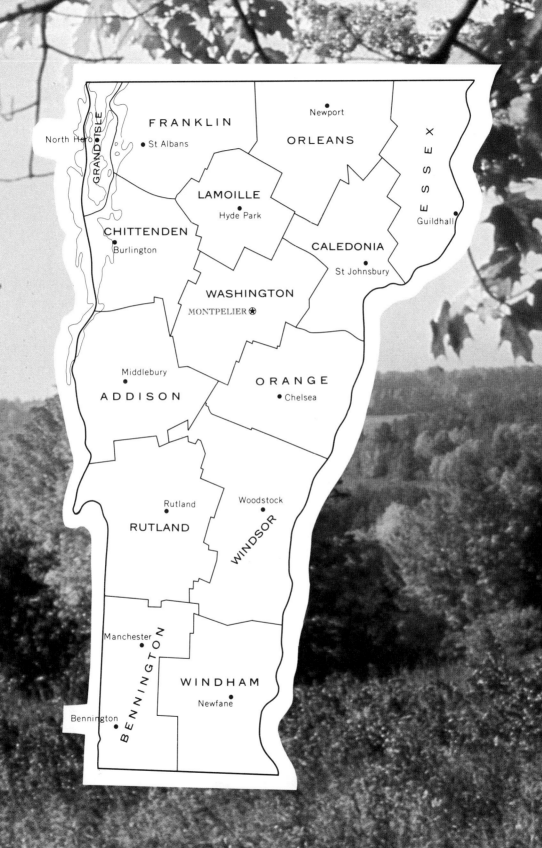

GRAND ISLE

North Hero

FRANKLIN

St Albans

Newport

ORLEANS

ESSEX

LAMOILLE

Hyde Park

Guildhall

CHITTENDEN

Burlington

CALEDONIA

St Johnsbury

WASHINGTON

MONTPELIER ✪

Middlebury

ORANGE

Chelsea

ADDISON

Rutland

Woodstock

RUTLAND

WINDSOR

Manchester

BENNINGTON

WINDHAM

Newfane

Bennington

The New
Enchantment of America
VERMONT

By Allan Carpenter

 CHILDRENS PRESS, CHICAGO

ACKNOWLEDGMENTS

For assistance in the preparation of the revised edition, the author thanks:
DONNA WELCH, Administrative Assistant, Vermont Travel Division, and DR. PAUL S. MASSIE, Assistant Director, Instructional Development Center, University of Vermont.

American Airlines—Anne Vitaliano, Director of Public Relations; *Capitol Historical Society*, Washington, D. C. ; *Newberry Library*, Chicago, Dr. Lawrence Towner, Director; *Northwestern University Library*, Evanston, Illinois; *United Airlines*—John P. Grember, Manager of Special Promotions; Joseph P. Hopkins, Manager, News Bureau; Carl Provorse, *Carpenter Publishing House.*

UNITED STATES GOVERNMENT AGENCIES: *Department of Agriculture*—Robert Hailstock, Jr., Photography Division, Office of Communication; Donald C. Schuhart, Information Division, Soil Conservation Service. *Army*—Doran Topolosky, Public Affairs Office, Chief of Engineers, Corps of Engineers. *Department of Interior*—Louis Churchville, Director of Communications; EROS Space Program—Phillis Wiepking, Community Affairs; Charles Withington, Geologist; Mrs. Ruth Herbert, Information Specialist; Bureau of Reclamation; National Park Service—Fred Bell and the individual sites; Fish and Wildlife Service—Bob Hines, Public Affairs Office. *Library of Congress*—Dr. Alan Fern, Director of the Department of Research; Sara Wallace, Director of Publications; Dr. Walter W. Ristow, Chief, Geography and Map Division; Herbert Sandborn, Exhibits Officer. *National Archives*—Dr. James B. Rhoads, Archivist of the United States; Albert Meisel, Assistant Archivist for Educational Programs; David Eggenberger, Publications Director; Bill Leary, Still Picture Reference; James Moore, Audio-Visual Archives. *United States Postal Service*—Herb Harris, Stamps Division.

For assistance in the preparation of the first edition, the author thanks:
Dr. Max W. Barrows, Director Instructional Services, State Department of Education, Montpelier; Graham S. Newell, Lyndon State College, Lyndonville; Weston A. Cate, Executive Secretary, Vermont Education Association; and the Vermont Development Department.

Illustrations on the preceding pages:
Cover photograph: Church in Newark, winter, Vermont Agency of Development and Community Affairs
Page 1: Commemorative stamps of historic interest
Pages 2-3: Adamant in the fall, Vermont Agency of Development and Community Affairs
Page 3: (Map) USDI Geological Survey
Pages 4-5: Lake Champlain and northern Vermont, EROS Space Photo, USDI Geological Survey, EROS Data Center

Project Editor, Revised Edition:
  Joan Downing
Assistant Editor, Revised Edition:
  Mary Reidy

Library of Congress Cataloging in Publication Data
Carpenter, John Allan, 1917-
  Vermont

  (His The new enchantment of America)
  SUMMARY: Presents the history, resources, economy, famous citizens, and points of interest in the Green Mountain State.
    1. Vermont—Juvenile literature.
[1. Vermont] I. Title. II. Series.
F49.3.C29   974.3   79-829
ISBN 0-516-04145-2

Contents

A True Story to Set the Scene

CAPTIVE MOTHER, DAUGHTER CAPTIVE

"A crowd of savages, fixed horribly for war, rushed furiously in. . . . I was led to the door, fainting and trembling . . . my three children were driven naked to the place where I stood. . . . Two savages laid hold of each of my arms, and hurried me through thorny thickets in a most unmerciful manner. I lost a shoe and suffered exceedingly."

Thus begins an incredible narrative of early America—a saga of suffering and endurance on a journey across Vermont. It is a story that portrays the perils of pioneer life and the ways and life of the Indians.

Captain and Mrs. James Johnson and their family lived in Charlestown, New Hampshire, just across the Connecticut River from present-day Vermont. At that time this was the most remote of frontier settlements. The French and English were almost constantly at war, and the French did not keep their Indian allies from attacking English settlers.

Mrs. Johnson wrote movingly of their dread: "The fears of the night were horrible beyond description, and even the light of day was far from dispelling painful anxiety. While looking from the windows of my log house, and seeing my neighbors tread cautiously by each hedge and hillock, lest some secreted savage might start forth to take their scalp, my fears would baffle description."

On August 30, 1754, her worst fears were realized when eleven Indians from Canada swept down and captured the Johnson family, along with Mrs. Johnson's fourteen-year-old sister and two neighbor men. Mrs. Johnson was expecting her fourth child at almost any moment.

"When the time came for us to prepare to march," she wrote, "I almost expired at the thought to leave my aged parents, brothers,

Except for the road, this section of Vermont woods probably looks much the same as it did when the Johnsons traveled through it with their Indian captors.

sisters and friends and travel with savages through a dismal forest to unknown regions in the alarming situation I then was in, with three small children, the oldest a boy six years old."

The Indians ferried their captives across the Connecticut on wooden rafts and set out across the wilderness of what was to become Vermont. Each of the captive party had a different Indian master. Indian tradition gave a prisoner to whichever Indian touched the captive first.

Capturing a neighbor's horse, named Scoggin, they let Mrs. Johnson ride most of the first day. At night the captives were tightly bound; the only food was watery gruel and the broth of a hawk the Indians had caught.

The next day Mrs. Johnson had to make signs to the Indians to stop so that the baby could be born. On the banks of a little creek the Indians "made a booth" where her husband and sister attended her. "About ten o'clock a daughter was born." When the first cry rang out, "my master looked into the booth and clapped his hands with joy." He was pleased to have an additional captive to sell or to ransom. The baby was named Captive Johnson.

"They [the Indians] brought a needle and two pins," Mrs. Johnson recalled, and some bark to tie the child's clothes . . . and a large wooden spoon to feed it with."

Soon they made Mrs. Johnson remount Scoggin, although she was about to faint, and they went off again. "Mr. Labarree [one of the neighbors]," she wrote, "kept the infant in his arms and preserved its life." Soon even the meal for gruel ran out and they could kill no game. At last the Indians killed and cooked the horse. Mrs. Johnson noted that they offered the prisoners the best parts: "An epicure could not have catered nicer slices, nor in that situation served them up with more neatness."

The next day "the marrow bones of old Scoggin were pounded for a soup and every root, both sweet and bitter that the woods afforded, was thrown in to give it a flavor." Then the party moved on once more for weary days of plodding. Now there was no mount for Mrs. Johnson. Finally, she wrote: "My power to move then failed, the world grew dark, and I dropped down. I had sight enough to see an

*When the Indians and their prisoners finally reached Lake Champlain
(above), the Johnsons were taken by canoe to French settlements.*

Indian lift his hatchet over my head, while my little son screamed—
'Ma'am do go, for they will kill you.' As I fainted, my last thought
was that I should presently be in the world of spirits. When I awoke,
my master was talking angrily with the savage who had threatened
my life." He did not want to lose his ransom.

For most of the rest of the journey, Mr. Johnson carried his wife,
although he was without shoes. Once Mr. Labarree dropped the baby
into a swift stream, but he managed to rescue her. As the terrible
ordeal continued, Mrs. Johnson wrote, "My wearied husband,
naked children, and helpless infant formed a scene that conveyed
severer pangs to my heart than all the sufferings I had endured
myself."

At last "after nine days of painful suffering," they reached Lake
Champlain, where the Indians had food and canoes to take them to
French settlements. The French treated them kindly but could not
offend their Indian allies by taking away their prisoners. Finally the
captives, worn almost as thin as skeletons, were brought to the
Indian village of St. Francis. Mrs. Johnson could find the kindness to
say, "The Indians had been surprisingly patient, and [we] often discovered tokens of humanity" in them. There was great celebration
in the Indian village when the warriors brought home their captives.

11

The captives were painted with vermillion war paint mixed with bear's grease, and were made to learn an Indian war dance and song.

Eventually all the prisoners except the boy were transferred to larger French cities. They were French prisoners of war for four years, living at times in dreadful prison holes. At last Mrs. Johnson was sent to England to try to arrange ransom. Her daughter, Captive, accompanied her.

Finally at 2:00 A.M. on New Year's Day, 1758, Captain and Mrs. Johnson were reunited at Charlestown. Later their son joined them; he had forgotten his parents and all his English and spoke only an Indian language. One daughter, who came later from Montreal, had been treated well and educated in French schools. She spoke only French.

While they were captive, Mrs. Johnson's father had been killed in another Indian raid. Captain Johnson was killed later in 1758 in the Battle of Ticonderoga.

Mrs. Johnson put her experiences into writing, and the *Narrative of the Captivity of Mrs. Johnson—containing an account of her suffering during four years with the Indians and French* was published in 1796.

Elizabeth Johnson later married John Hastings and they had seven children. Until the last two years of her life Mrs. Hastings lived on the same spot where the Indians had taken her captive. Her daughter Captive married Colonel George Kimball.

Mr. Labarree died in 1803 at the age of seventy-nine; Captive Johnson Kimball attended to him in his last illness as tenderly as he had cared for her during her first precarious days of life. Captive was the third European child born in what is now Vermont, and the strange circumstances of her birth have given her a secure place in the history of colonial New England.

Elizabeth Johnson Hastings died November 27, 1810, at age eighty-one, after a lifetime filled with hardship and disappointment.

The extraordinary narrative of the Johnsons' capitivity was republished three times later, the last time on August 30, 1904, on the 150th anniversary of the raid. It provides us with a simple yet powerful demonstration of the strength of the human spirit under the most incredible hardships, in the wilderness of early Vermont.

Lay of the Land

"MY MOUNTAIN GREENERY HOME"

A strange procession wound its way up the mountainside. Its leader was a Connecticut clergyman, the Reverend Samuel Peters. He was followed on that day in 1763 by a number of the proprietors of nearby townships. When the group reached the top of Killington Peak, the Reverend Mr. Peters looked around, admiring the tremendous view of rolling verdant hills. He broke a bottle of spirits soundly across one of the rocks and declaimed in loud tones, "I christen thee Vert-mont, a new name worthy of the Athenians and ancient Spartans, in token that her mountains and hills shall be ever green, and shall never die."

Whether or not such a dramatic christening ever took place may never be known. Most historians doubt it; however, the Reverend Mr. Peters always claimed that he had given Vermont its name in this unique way. *Vert* is the French word meaning green and *mont* means mountain, so that Vermont comes from the French phrase meaning "green mountain."

Later, Pastor Peters complained bitterly that the letter "t" had been left out of the name. He said the word *ver* means maggots, so that the present name means literally a "mountain of worms."

Whatever its origin or exact meaning, the very name of Vermont denotes the most important single feature of the area's geography. Those green mountains have left their stamp on the character of the people and the very destiny of the state.

Two mountain ranges—the massive scenic Green Mountains and the lower Taconics—and two ranges of high hills—the Red Sandrock Hills and the Granite Hills—make up the major highlands of the state. The outline of Mount Mansfield in the Green Mountains is compared to a human face, with the nose upturned and the lofty chin forming the highest point in the state, 4,393 feet (1,339 meters) above sea level. Other major Green Mountains are Killington, 4,241 feet (1,293 meters); Mount Ellen, 4,135 feet (1,260 meters); and Camel's Hump, 4,083 feet (1,244 meters).

Although the mountains do not rise very high above sea level, their vertical slope is greater than that of many of the mountains in the western United States. There is a rise of 4,000 feet (1,220 meters) from the bank of the Winooski River to the summit of Camel's Hump, only 4 miles (6.4 kilometers) away.

The lower Taconic Mountains begin in Massachusetts and extend from the southwest corner of Vermont to about Sudbury. The Red Sandrock Hills range along Lake Champlain from St. Albans to Addison. The Granite Hills, east of the Green Mountains, stretch from about mid-state to Canada.

IN ANCIENT TIMES

Geologists state that the Green Mountains are a very old range, infinitely older than the White Mountains to the east or the Adirondacks to the west.

Thousands of years ago the Cambrian Sea washed across the area that is now the Champlain Valley. This was due to a lowering of the valley floor. When the land rose the sea vanished, only to sink and flood again centuries later. At various times, forces below the earth twisted and folded the layers of the land until they became mountain ranges, such as the granite batholiths forming the Granite Hills. A later action—the Appalachian Revolution—forced up a great range all along the present eastern part of what is now the United States, raising the Green Mountains as one of its parts. Sometimes peaks were formed when layers of softer material eroded away.

At times in the ancient past, the Vermont area was almost tropical in climate. Later the great glaciers rearranged everything in their paths. The tremendous weight of the glaciers caused the land to sink at least 500 feet (150 meters). When the last of the glaciers melted, much of the area was under water. Prehistoric Lake Champlain covered a vast area to a great depth. Gradually the land rose again, relieved of its weight of ice. In places where depressions had been gouged out by the movement of the glaciers or where the glaciers had left natural dams called moraines, lakes were formed.

14

The story of these ancient times is learned entirely from the rocks and fossils left behind. A fossil coral reef on Isle La Motte looks strangely out of place as it rises to a height of seven feet (two meters) in quiet pasture land remote from any ocean. Yet the reef is a reminder that the seas at one time visited this region. It is thought to be the oldest coral reef in the world.

LAND OF OMPOMPANOOSUC AND MEMPHREMAGOG

Vermont is bordered by Canada (Quebec), New Hampshire, Massachusetts, and New York. The most impressive portions of these boundaries are formed by bodies of water. One of the best-known lakes in the United States is Lake Champlain, and about two thirds of this important lake lies within Vermont.

Depending on the exact definition of a lake there are from one hundred to four hundred lakes in Vermont, with Lake Bomoseen the largest natural body of water entirely within the state. Other lakes include Memphremagog ("beautiful waters" in an Indian language), only a quarter in Vermont and the rest in Canada; Lake Whitingham; glacial Lake Willoughby, 600 feet (180 meters) deep; and Sterling Pond near Stowe, with its placid waters at an altitude of 3,200 feet (975 meters), reflecting the sun.

The Connecticut River may be called the most important river touching Vermont, but it is not "in" Vermont. By judgment of the United States Supreme Court, all of the Connecticut River between Vermont and New Hampshire belongs to the latter state, and Vermont begins only at the western edge of the river. Vermont has not found this a great loss, although New Hampshire gets the revenue from several hydroelectric power dams on the river. Vermonters still enjoy the river, and New Hampshire is obliged to pay the upkeep for all of the bridges.

Three rivers cut through the Green Mountains and flow into Lake Champlain—the Winooski (once called the Onion River), Lamoille, and Missisquoi. Otter Creek is the longest river within the state. The Mad, Ompompanoosuc, and Ottauquechee are other rivers.

CLIMATE

The growing season in Vermont ranges from 120 days in the Connecticut Valley to 150 in the Lake Champlain Valley. Winters in the state are described as "crisp but generally not uncomfortable." Periods of extreme cold are usually brief, and the low humidity makes the temperature seem less severe. Summers are warm, but the evenings are delightfully cool.

Glacial Lake Willoughby, one of the most beautiful in the world, is often compared to Lake Lucerne in Switzerland.

Footsteps on the Land

Relatively little is known about the prehistoric inhabitants of what is now Vermont. Their picture writing, called pictographs, are found at such places as Bellows Falls. At Orwell were found graves containing red ochre buried with the dead. The remains of these prehistoric people, named the Red Paint Indians by anthropologists, have been unearthed throughout New England.

When the first Europeans came into the area, there were very few permanent Indian settlements in what is now Vermont. However, the Indians used the region for many purposes. At Bristol Pond spearheads and arrowheads were chipped from the local rocks. The area was popular for hunting and fishing, and when in the region temporarily, the Indians lived in tepees rather than in their permanent type of houses. A small amount of farming may have been done in a few places.

Most importantly the region served as a vital transportation route between north and south. The Algonquin Indians struggled for many years to keep this corridor from falling into the hands of the Iroquois to the southwest. Some Indian settlements were established eventually in what is now Vermont. The oldest and largest of these was near Swanton. There was also a permanent settlement at Newbury. Important relics of Indian settlement have been found at Bellows Falls and Chimney Point.

THE FRENCH WERE FIRST

French leader and explorer Samuel de Champlain stood at Chimney Point on July 30, 1609, and viewed with pride and pleasure the great body of water he had discovered on the fourth of July that year. Here he named the inland sea for himself; it has been Lake Champlain ever since.

There is no proof that any Europeans had ever set foot in what is now Vermont at an earlier time. In 1835 a lead cylinder was found on the banks of the Missisquoi River. Inside was a paper which read

Statue of Champlain on Isle La Motte

"Nov. 29 A.D.1564—This is the solem day I must now die this is the 90th day since we lef the Ship all have Parished and on the Banks of this River I die to farewell may future Posteritye know our end— John Graye." At its discovery this poignant message's writer was thought to have been a member of the Martin Frobisher expedition. However, most experts now believe that this message from a legendary sailor was a forgery and a hoax. Champlain is still secure in his reputation as the discoverer of Vermont.

In the Lake Champlain region, Champlain and his Algonquin allies fought a battle with the Iroquois. This was the first time the Iroquois had been faced with enemies who used rifles. They were defeated badly. These proud Indians who considered themselves masters of the continent would not forget. The Iroquois never forgave the French; the Iroquois waged war until, with their English allies, they drove the French from the continent more than 150 years later.

Although Champlain's discovery gave the French claim to the area, they were slow to follow it up. The French did not establish their first settlement in what is now Vermont until 1666.

In that year three hundred French soldiers under Captain de La Motte hewed a fortress out of the wilderness on an island in Lake Champlain. The island now bears Captain de La Motte's name. The

18

scene must have been a strange one as the party's shirtsleeved aristocrats directed the labors of their men in this remote wilderness, while the dark-robed, solemn Jesuits attended to their duties. Here, at what was called Fort Ste. Anne, the first Catholic Mass in present-day Vermont was celebrated. Fort Ste. Anne was established to defend the French interests against the Mohawk Iroquois tribe, but was soon abandoned.

The longest-lived French settlement in Vermont was at present-day Swanton. Here Jesuit priests taught the St. Francis Indians. Under the direction of the Jesuit Fathers, the Indians built a chapel. Much later, after the French were finally driven out of the region, the St. Francis Indians, in devotion for their chapel, moved it stone by stone to their new home in Canada.

THE ENGLISH WERE NEXT

For almost a hundred years until about 1760 the French and English fought a series of wars. The French were helped by their Algonquin allies and the English by the feared Iroquois.

In 1690 the English built a fort at Chimney Point, and a few settlers drifted in from western Massachusetts settlements. The colonists in what is now southern Vermont lived in terror of Indian attacks, and in 1724 Fort Dummer, near the present site of Brattleboro, was built as an outpost to warn the colonists of the approach of their Indian enemies. Fort Dummer is usually considered the first permanent European settlement in what is now Vermont.

The French and Indian War, the last and heaviest fighting between England and France in the New World, began in 1756. The scattered settlements in the western frontier—western Massachusetts, Vermont, and eastern New York—suffered terribly from scalping raids by the St. Francis Indians. To help stop these raids Major Robert Rogers led a daring raid on the St. Francis village, the Indian headquarters far to the north in Canada.

Major Rogers, with two hundred men uniformed in green buckskins, left his boats and major supplies at Missisquoi Bay on

Lake Champlain and set out on the difficult overland journey. Messengers soon brought him news that his boats and supplies had been captured, and that a large French force was in pursuit. However, Rogers kept this unhappy news from his men and pushed on.

On the night of October 4, 1759, the Indians of St. Francis were holding a great ceremony of dancing and feasting when Rogers and his Rangers reached the village. At four in the morning the Rangers attacked the sleeping settlement. The St. Francis Indians had treated the English settlers of New England cruelly, and Rogers had orders to show the braves no mercy but to spare the women and children. As the dawn's light came, the Rangers were so enraged at the sight of hundreds of white scalps hanging from poles in the village that they began to slaughter men, women, and children. The Rangers lost only one man in the battle; two hundred Indians were killed and twenty were taken prisoner.

Pursued by Indians bent on revenge, Rogers and his Rangers made a remarkable flight back to English settlements. Suffering terribly from hunger, they counted on meeting a rescue party from New Hampshire, but they missed them near what is now East Barnet. Several of the men died there of starvation. Rogers taught the others how to get nourishment from lily roots and ground nuts; they made a raft and Rogers and three other men set out down the Connecticut River to bring help from Charlestown, New Hampshire. Their skeletonlike comrades watched them leave from shore.

At White River Falls, where the White River meets the Connecticut, they were forced to abandon their raft and walk around the falls. Here, they built another raft by burning down trees, then burning the trees further to the proper length and lashing them together. Fortunately, Captain Ogden managed to shoot a partridge, which helped to sustain them.

When Rogers and his three companions came to Ottauquechee Rapids, it seemed impossible to get the crude raft through the falls, and yet they knew they would not have the strength to build still another raft below the rapids. Tireless and fearless, Rogers walked to the foot of the falls, and his men let the raft loose to plunge down the rapids. Fortunately, it held together; Rogers swam into the swift current, clambered onto the raft, and brought it to shore.

Finally the party reached help at Charlestown, and Rogers went back up the Connecticut River to rescue his starving comrades. In spite of the battle, the pursuit by the Indians, and the hardship of the journey, only fifty of the original party of two hundred had been lost. This epic journey has been described in *Northwest Passage,* by Kenneth Roberts.

The deeds of Rogers and his Rangers are only one part of the conflict that raged halfway across the continent. Gradually the British gained the upper hand.

When the Treaty of Paris was signed in 1763, England had won the continent, and the French had lost the century-long battle to keep their hold in North America.

"GREEN MOUNTAIN BOYS AGAINST THE WORLD"

The next periods in Vermont history were unique in the annals of the United States.

In 1741 King George II of England issued a proclamation giving New Hampshire all territory extending "till it meets with our other governments." However, the New York boundary had not been defined exactly. According to Timothy Walker in 1778, "The King had never told his Governor of New Hampshire, in express terms, how far west he should go, and there stop, nor his Governor of New York how far east he should go and then cease." Governor Benning Wentworth of New Hampshire assumed that New Hampshire would extend the same distance west as Massachusetts and Connecticut, including all of Vermont.

Governor George Clinton of New York claimed that the original New York grant to the Duke of York included "all the land from the west side of the Conectecutte River. . . ."

The two governors agreed to leave the decision to the king, and in the meantime the French and Indian War stopped interest in the matter. Nevertheless, Governor Wentworth granted land in the disputed area; after 1759 he made as many as sixty grants in a single year. The earliest grant in what is now Vermont was Westminster, probably in 1735. In 1749 Bennington was the first town chartered by New Hampshire west of the Connecticut River.

In 1764, George III made a decision; he proclaimed that the Connecticut River was the boundary of New Hampshire, and the lands to the west (including all of Vermont) belonged to New York. Most of the settlers in present-day Vermont had come from New England, and they were living on New Hampshire grants. As soon as New York was declared the owner, New York began to give grants in the area, many of them covering the same land as the New Hampshire grants.

The grant holders from New Hampshire, naturally, were distressed. Most of them could not purchase their property from New York even if they recognized the New York title. A long and bitter struggle followed, growing more violent as the causes of the dispute deepened.

In 1770, during this period of uncertainty, the famous Green Mountain Boys were organized under the colorful leadership of self-taught, self-made Ethan Allen. Other prominent members of the group were Seth Warner, captain of the Bennington Company; Remember Baker; Micah Vail; and Thomas Rowley. Rowley, the poet of the Green Mountain Boys, was celebrated for his wit. They met in Bennington at the Green Mountain Tavern, owned by Stephen Fay. Above the tavern sign they placed a stuffed mountain lion (catamount), facing New York, with his teeth bared in defiance. In all ways possible they terrorized those who tried to claim New York land grants. The "high chair" treatment was a popular "cure" for New Yorkers. The offender was tied to a chair and hoisted high in the air by ropes where he was suspended above a jeering crowd. When a Colonel Reid of New York sent Scottish emigrants to make homes on his claims in Vergennes, a band of a hundred Green Mountain Boys set fire to their huts, destroyed their gristmill, and drove the settlers away.

These and other activities of the Ethan Allen militia were considered highly proper by the holders of New Hampshire grants. They spoke of "the Green Mountain Boys against the world." However, they were known as the Bennington Mob by the New Yorkers. Benjamin Spencer wrote to a friend in 1772: "One Ethan Allen hath brought from Connecticut twelve or fifteen of the most blackguard fellows he can get, doubly armed in order to protect him."

A year later, Allen and his boys brought Spencer to a mock trial in his own dooryard. Upon finding him "guilty" they ripped the roof from his house "with great shouting and much noise and tumult." After making Spencer take an oath of allegiance to their cause, they surprisingly replaced the roof of his house. Other New Yorkers did not fare so well. Many houses were burned and numberless bare backs were beaten with lashes cut from beech trees.

New York officials did not stand by idly. In 1771 they sent a force of three hundred men under Sheriff Ten Eyck to capture the Breakenridge farm near Bennington. When this news spread across the countryside, Bennington men grabbed any weapon they could find, including pitchforks, scythes, and swords as well as muskets, and drove the invaders back after a scuffle at the old covered bridge near the farm.

This life-sized bronze statue of a catamount in Bennington is a reminder of the one on the sign at the tavern where Ethan Allen and his Green Mountain Boys met.

Ethan Allen came to be known as the Robin Hood of Vermont. He and Warner, Baker, and Robert Cochran all had prices put on their heads by the state of New York. Some historians have called them outlaws, while others have labeled them heroes. Whatever the personal opinion, the Green Mountain Boys managed to break the hold of New York on the area and start Vermont on the road to statehood.

THE REVOLUTION

The people of Vermont were more concerned with their own problems than with the political controversies that would soon lead to war with England. However, as early as October 10, 1774, a declaration of independence was written by the people of Chester, stating that "all the acts of British Parliament tending to take away Rights of Freedom ought not to be obeyed."

At Westminster on March 13, 1775, a group of armed men of the community took control of the courthouse from the New York authorities. County officials loyal to New York brought in a force under the command of the sheriff. Shots were fired into the courthouse, and two men, William French and Daniel Houghton, were killed. This Westminster Massacre has sometimes been called the first battle of the Revolution. Now it is generally agreed that it had very little to do with the coming war or its causes since the protest was against the government of New York and not that of the king, although these officers held final authority from the crown. Even so, the tombstone of William French declares that he was shot "by the hands of cruel ministerial tools of George ye 3rd."

More important in the Revolutionary cause was the strange and unique triumph of Vermont's own Ethan Allen. In their favorite tavern in Bennington, Allen and his boys plotted the seemingly impossible capture of Fort Ticonderoga on the New York side of Lake Champlain. They were joined by an unwanted partner, the strange and later tragic Benedict Arnold. Allen and Arnold disagreed on who should lead the attack. Arnold had been commissioned by

24

When Ethan Allen and the Green Mountain Boys arrived to capture Fort Ticonderoga, they found that the British at the stronghold were sleeping.

the Continental Congress, but the New Hampshire grants (Vermont) had not recognized the Congress. At length, Arnold and Allen agreed to share the command.

Gershom Beach of Whiting walked 64 miles (103 kilometers) in twenty-four hours to gather the Green Mountain Boys for the attack, and they set off—a force of only about eighty-three—to capture a stronghold that once withstood an assault by fifteen thousand soldiers. After overcoming one sentry, they found the British garrison sleeping. In his *Narrative of the Capture of Ticonderoga,* Allen says he called on the British commander to surrender "In the name of the Great Jehovah and the Continental Congress." As one critic has remarked, he made this request "in spite of the fact that he held a commission from neither source."

The capture of the strongest fort then on the continent proved to be a great inspiration to the struggling forces of the American Revolution. Later that year Seth Warner and his fighting band captured Crown Point just north of Fort Ticonderoga.

In the summer of 1776, under the direction of brilliant, unpredictable Benedict Arnold, the people of Vermont used the forest along the shore of Lake Champlain to build a fleet for defense against an almost overwhelming British fleet on the lake. Arnold led these newly built ships into the Battle of Valcour Island, in New York waters. After damaging the British fleet greatly, he deceived the Bri-

This painting depicts the capture of Fort Ticonderoga by Ethan Allen and the Green Mountain Boys on May 10, 1775.

Painting of the Green Mountain Boys of Vermont on Lake Champlain

tish with a decoy so that most of his ships could escape. Then he ran his flagship and four smaller ships aground on Arnold Bay near Panton and set them on fire—with their flags flying—to keep them out of British hands. This battle has been called an American defeat, but the British suffered such heavy losses that their offensive from the north had to be delayed for a year. This gave the Americans time to prepare their defenses.

On July 6, 1777, British General John Burgoyne recaptured Fort Ticonderoga. American General Arthur St. Clair abandoned it without a struggle, hurried across the float bridge to Mt. Independence, and then fled toward Castleton by way of Hubbardton. The British followed and the next day caught up with St. Clair's rear guard at Hubbardton. This rear guard was commanded by Colonel Seth Warner.

Warner's ragged army of farmers was cooking breakfast when the British attacked; they ran for cover and fought Indian style. For a time it appeared that the Americans had beaten the proud British, but the British brought up their hired German reinforcements, and the remaining Warner troops turned south again after what has been called "one of the most successful rear-guard actions in American annals." Warner's men had inflicted so many enemy casualties that the attacking forces retreated to Fort Ticonderoga. According to the Vermont Board of Historic Sites, the British plan to "seize stores and property at Castleton and Rutland and to wreak havoc on the main American army ahead was completely upset. Though a short battle involving no more than 2,000 men, its significance was quite out of proportion to its size. The first successful resistance to Burgoyne, it forged the first link in a chain of military events leading to the capitulation of his once splendid Royal Army at Saratoga, two months later."

The Battle of Hubbardton was the only battle of the American Revolution to take place on the soil of what is now Vermont.

The Battle of Bennington in September 1777 actually was fought across the border in New York. However, Vermont men played a most important part in this battle. General Burgoyne had heard that quantities of badly needed supplies, especially horses, were stored at Bennington. He sent the following bold orders to Colonel Baum: "Mount your dragoons . . . send me 1300 horses . . . seize Bennington . . . cross mountains to Rockingham and Brattleborough . . . try affections of country . . . take hostages . . . meet me a fortnight hence in Albany."

The arrogant general never reached Albany, except later as a prisoner. Fortunately, Colonel John Stark reached Bennington before Baum. Stark, aided by Colonel Seth Warner, moved to meet the enemy in New York, west of Bennington. He supposedly called out the famous words, "There are the Red Coats and they are ours, or this night Molly Stark sleeps a widow!" Baum's troops were almost beaten when German reinforcements arrived for the British. Stark reportedly was ready to let his tired men fall back, but Seth Warner persuaded him against this. They even had to teach their

Colonel John Stark, who led Revolutionary troops to victory in the Battle of Bennington.

inexperienced soldiers how to fire their captured cannon. At the critical moment, 350 of Warner's Green Mountain Boys arrived, the only fresh troops on the scene, and the tide was turned; the German reinforcements fled in a rout.

Molly Stark did not become a widow that day, and more than two hundred British were killed and six hundred taken prisoner. American forces led by Horatio Gates attacked the crippled British forces a month later at Saratoga, forcing Burgoyne's surrender on October 17, 1777. This defeat ended British hopes to isolate New England from the rest of the colonies, and proved to be a turning point in the war.

Before the Battle of Bennington the British had sent a message to the Catamount Tavern requesting that dinner be ready after their triumphal capture of the town. As the British prisoners shuffled along the street, bleeding from their wounds, their uniforms torn and stained, the inn's owner, Stephen Fay, mockingly made a low bow and called out, "Gentlemen, the dinner you ordered is ready." Fay had five sons fighting in the Battle of Bennington, and one of them, John, was killed. His death inspired the Bennington volunteers to one of the important victories of the day.

TERRORS AT HOME

Those who remained at home in Vermont suffered terribly from raids by the Indian allies of the British. These war parties swept down the historic raiding route from Canada, burning, killing, and taking prisoners. Many homes were equipped with secret hiding closets or rooms to provide some protection during Indian attacks.

One such Indian attack was on the cabin of John Kilburn at Shrewsbury on August 17, 1775. Kilburn, his family, and a neighbor and his family held out from noon until sunset against a throng of Indians "as thick as grasshoppers." Kilburn survived to see the fourth generation of his descendants enjoy the land he fought to save.

Hannah Hunter Handy of South Royalton was captured by Indian raiders in 1780. One of them knocked her down with the butt of a rifle, but she struggled to her feet. A friendly Waubanakee Indian carried her across the White River, and she hurried off alone to the enemy camp to find her children. One by one she tried to rescue her own and the other captured children and each time was struck down. Finally the Indians were so impressed with her courage that she was allowed to go home with nine of the young captives.

In the same raid, Phineas Parkhurst was wounded, but he rode off madly on his horse to warn the other White River Valley residents as far away as Lebanon, New Hampshire.

In the worst of all the Indian raids on Vermont, three hundred Indians under English Lieutenant Horton terrorized the valley from Tunbridge to Royalton in October 1780. They plundered and burned as they went, and Royalton was reduced to ashes. The twenty-six prisoners were hauled back to Canada where they were said to have been sold like cattle for eight dollars each. One of the prisoners, Zadock Steele, wrote a long and interesting account of his captivity.

At last, of course, the American Revolution, with all its suffering and hardship, drew to a close. It had brought with it for Vermont an entirely new set of opportunities and problems.

Yesterday and Today

THE REPUBLIC OF VERMONT

The future of present-day Vermont had been partly decided in a series of conventions. In 1776 the Green Mountain Boys and other patriots met in Kent's taproom at Dorset and declared the state to be independent. A January 1777 convention at Westminster provided for the establishment of the free state of New Connecticut.

On June 4, 1777, a group of seventy-two delegates from the New Hampshire grants met at Windsor to frame a constitution for a new and independent state. The constitution was ready on July 8, and the delegates met in a Windsor tavern. Just at that moment, news came of the Battle of Hubbardton. In the excitement most of the delegates were ready to dash off, and the constitution might never have been signed.

However, a violent thunderstorm kept them confined to the hall long enough to approve the constitution, and the independent state of Vermont was "born amidst a baptism of thunder, lightning, and rain." Dr. Thomas Young of Philadelphia, a close friend of Ethan Allen, had advised the delegates to change the name of New Connecticut to Vermont.

The constitution of Vermont was the first in the nation to offer the right to vote to all adult males and to prohibit slavery. The bill of rights of the constitution declared that no one of legal age "ought to be holden by law to serve any person as a servant or slave, or apprentice."

Thomas Chittenden was elected governor on March 3, 1778, in the first election under the constitution. On March 12 of that same year, the first session of the legislature was held. This legislature had only one house (known as the unicameral system) instead of two.

From 1777 until 1791 Vermont operated as a completely independent republic. Vermonters sang:

> We owe no allegiance, we bow to no throne,
> Our ruler is law, and the law is our own.

However, the new government was not recognized by either the Continental Congress, the governing body of the other struggling colonies, or by New York. Many residents of the state also refused to recognize the new government. Some were loyal to New York while many, known as Tories, remained loyal to England and the king.

The struggle between the colonial partisans was especially fierce in Guilford, where in 1772 the residents had voted that Guilford was a part of the county of Cumberland in New York. But as time went by, many regretted this; according to one authority for about fifteen years "the town was literally in a state of continuous civil war." Each group elected its own town officials. Each side held its own heavily armed town meetings. The New York records for May 1782 read: "Then the people met in general and voted to stand against the pretended state of Vermont."

Ethan Allen came to Guilford in 1783 and proclaimed, "I, Ethan Allen, declare that unless the people of Guilford peaceably submit to the authority of Vermont, the town shall be made as desolate as were the cities of Sodom and Gomorrah by God." With his one hundred Green Mountain Boys, Allen managed to collect taxes for Vermont and establish the authority of the Vermont sheriff.

STATEHOOD

During the later years of the Revolution, Vermont seemed almost withdrawn from the conflict. The neighboring states resented what they felt was lack of support for their cause. However, it has been said that Vermont's "near-neutrality" may have kept the British from trying to launch later invasions from Canada.

Many in Vermont hoped to join the United States, but there were frequent misunderstandings and Vermont seemed to become more independent, carrying out all the operations of a sovereign state, such as the minting of coins under the direction of Reuben Harmon. These Vermont coins are now highly valued as collector's items.

George Washington at one time felt it might be necessary to send troops into Vermont to bring it into line. In 1783 he wrote a famous letter on this subject to the president of Congress, then operating under the Articles of Confederation. However, Vermont became more stable, gained the respect of its neighbors, and the quarrel with New York over property rights was settled in 1790 for $30,000. In January 1791, Vermont adopted the Constitution of the United States. Congress unanimously accepted Vermont as the fourteenth state, on March 4 of that year. Vermont had the distinction of being the first state added to the Union after the original thirteen. What had been a wilderness with three hundred inhabitants in 1760 had become a state of the Union with almost ninety thousand people.

In 1805 Montpelier was selected as the capital of Vermont. As early as 1808 the steamboat *Vermont* was operating on Lake Champlain. Modern progress had reached the wilderness.

During this period Congress declared an embargo that made it illegal to buy from or sell goods to Britain or its colonies. Vermont became a favorite route for smugglers. Such a large volume of illegal goods and cattle flowed both ways through the pass near Cambridge, beside majestic Mount Mansfield, that it became known as Smuggler's Notch, and still bears that name.

Many thrilling tales are told of gunfights between smugglers and the border guards, and of other smuggling activities. One smuggler fell through the ice near Alburg. His clothes froze so stiffly that he could not rise and had to let his horse drag him across the lake to the town. One of the most famous incidents was the capture of the smuggling ship *Black Snake* near Burlington. Several men were killed in the fight over this boat, and Captain Daniel Farrington, commander of the Canadian border patrol, was wounded. Cyrus Dean of the *Black Snake* was sentenced to be hanged. On November 11, 1808, a crowd of ten thousand persons gathered in Burlington to view the first public hanging in the state.

ANOTHER WAR

Even during the War of 1812 with Britain, the smuggling continued. In 1814, according to Sir George Prevost, Canada's gover-

Macdonough's Victory on Lake Champlain,
September 11, 1814, *by Currier and Ives.*

nor-general, "two-thirds of the army in Canada are at this moment eating beef provided by American contractors, drawn principally from the states of Vermont and New York." American General Izard was of the opinion that "were it not for these supplies, the British forces in Canada would soon be suffering from famine."

Loyal Vermonters, however, were alert to the dangers of an invasion from Canada. Governor Martin Chittenden, the son of Vermont's first governor, gave a controversial order to the state's militia to return to Vermont from Plattsburgh, New York, where it had been stationed.

Lieutenant Thomas Macdonough was ordered to Vermont to command the fleet on Lake Champlain, which he found to be a "poor, forlorn-looking squadron." He made winter quarters for his fleet at Shelburne in 1812-1813, and there were small battles on the lake. Macdonough, determined to enlarge his fleet, established a shipyard at Vergennes on Otter Creek. Vermont's master builders ripped apart the state's great timbers and built a fleet in record time. Macdonough's flagship, the U.S.S. *Saratoga*, was built in only forty days.

These Vermont-built ships played the key part in the Battle of Plattsburgh, in September 1814, which gave the Americans control of Lake Champlain and prevented Vermont's invasion. Vermont men also had an important role in the land battle that accompanied the naval fight. Without these Vermont contributions, the Americans probably would have lost the battle. Old Fort Cassin was used to keep the British from going up Otter Creek and destroying the half-finished ships.

A PERIOD BETWEEN

The most terrible winter in Vermont's history struck in 1816. There was killing frost in every month of the year, three-foot (one-meter) snowdrifts in June, and snow well into July and August. With wry humor the people labeled the year "1800 and froze to death." More grimly, it was known as the "famine year." Practically no crops were harvested. Livestock died for want of feed, and people were reduced to eating wild turnips, small game, and other makeshift meals.

One of the exciting events of the period in Vermont was the visit of the revered Marquis de Lafayette in 1825. Staying overnight at Montpelier, he offered a toast, "To Vermont, Montpelier, and the Green Mountains, from which was echoed early, and valiantly supported, the Republican cry for Independence and Freedom." In Vermont, Lafayette heard how Colonel William Barton of Barton had been jailed for a long period for a minor debt because of the jealousy of some rivals in the area. Recalling Barton as a worthy soldier, the Marquis at once arranged to have him set free. This interest in old friends was typical of Lafayette.

In the 1820s and early 1830s a strange movement against the Masons gained its greatest strength in Vermont. Vermont elected an anti-Masonic governor in 1831, and was the only state to vote for the anti-Masonic candidate for president in the election of 1832.

Other important events in Vermont's political history were the formation of Lamoille County in 1835—the last county created in the state—and the changing of the state legislature to the two-house (bicameral) system in 1836. When famed statesman-orator Daniel Webster spoke at Stratton in 1840 he drew a crowd of fifteen thousand people.

In the war with Mexico in 1846 Vermonters Captain Kimball and Sergeant Major Fairbanks were the first to lower the Mexican flag from the Bishop's Palace at Chapultepec in Mexico. Truman Ransom left the presidency of Norwich University to fight in the war and became a hero, dying in the assault on Chapultepec.

Most Vermont residents opposed the war; they felt its main result would be the addition of more slave states to the United States. Although there had never been any slaves in Vermont, the people were bitterly opposed to slavery. Almost every year the Vermont legislature passed resolutions condemning slavery and sent copies of these to each of the Southern slave states. The enraged Southern states responded. The Georgia legislature promised to send its answer to the Vermont governor enclosed in a lead bullet, accompanied by a length of rope suitable for hanging. Another Georgia resolution asked the president to dig a ditch around Vermont so that "the thing could be sailed away on the ocean."

Vermont's hatred for slavery grew until the state was regarded as the symbol for the abolitionists—those who wanted to abolish slavery. In 1803, Judge Theopholis Harrington had been asked to rule for a slave owner in a runaway slave case, but he told the owner his title was not good. The indignant owner showed the judge that it was legal according to all the laws and asked the judge what else he needed to press his claim. "A bill of sale, sir, from God Almighty!" the judge roared back.

Vermonters put their antislavery ideas into practice by operating many stations on the underground railroad, the route taken by slaves escaping to Canada. Its border with Canada made Vermont particularly important to the route's success. Fair Haven and St. Albans were major stations on the underground railroad.

FIGHTING FOR THE UNION

When the nation finally went to war in 1861, Vermont contributed 34,328 men to the Union army. This was a very large percentage of the state's men of military age, and an alarming percentage of Vermont's men lost their lives. This is illustrated by the fact that Stowe lost 45 of the 60 men who fought in the Civil War. Altogether 5,128 Vermont men were killed in the conflict.

Many Vermonters played interesting and important roles in the war. Jacob Collamer of Woodstock, a United States senator during the war, was a close advisor of President Abraham Lincoln. In July 1861 Collamer wrote and introduced the bill that gave Lincoln his first powers to carry on the Civil War. General George Stannard was born near Georgia Center, Vermont. When Confederate General George Pickett launched his famous charge in the Battle of Gettysburg, General Stannard threw his forces against Pickett in a counterattack that proved to be one of the battle's turning points. Stannard's forces, the Sixteenth Vermont Regiment, also turned back a later attack by a brigade from Florida. General Stannard was wounded in this charge, but he refused to leave his command until his replacement had arrived.

Probably the best-known private of the war was William Scott, born near Groton. He became known as the Sleeping Sentinel because he had fallen asleep on sentinel duty and was sentenced to death. The men of his company appealed to President Lincoln. They told how on the night before Scott had stood sentry duty for a sick friend, and when he had to stand a second night's duty without rest, he fell asleep.

The president visited Scott in prison and gave him a personal pardon. Lincoln was severely criticized by those who said that such "soft" actions would cripple army discipline. However, Scott continued to serve his country and died on the battlefield at Lee's Mill, Virginia.

One of the most bizarre of all the engagements of the Civil War was "fought" in Vermont. At 3:00 P.M. on October 19, 1864, the town of St. Albans was going quietly about its regular business when a group of twenty-two fully uniformed Southern soldiers under Lieutenant Bennett Young suddenly appeared as if from nowhere. Groups of them raided the town's three banks simultaneously, made off with $200,000, killed one townsman, and wounded a few others. Then the raiders seized horses and dashed out of town, setting fire to Sheldon Bridge as they went. As the news of the attack spread across the state its size was magnified, and all of Vermont was alive to the possibility of a Southern attack from Canada.

It was discovered later that this small group had slipped into town individually in civilian clothes to escape detection and then had assembled for a carefully planned attack. Lieutenant Young and his men escaped to nearby Canada, and Canada refused to turn them over to the United States or to do anything about recovering the money. (Canada later compensated St. Albans' banks with $80,000.) A motion picture, *The Raid,* dramatized this unique event in Vermont history. This has been called "the most northerly engagement of the war," but some naval skirmishes off Alaska probably deserve that distinction.

Chester A. Arthur (left) became president of the United States in 1881.

A MODERN STATE

Canada and Vermont played a part in another strange series of events after the war was over. A group of Irish patriots known as the Fenians planned to strike at the British Empire by capturing Canada. Vermont was one of the most important centers of operation for the Fenians, and some people of the state may have been sympathetic to them. In one of the largest and last of these attempts, more than two thousand Fenians assembled near Franklin under "General" John O'Neil. They attacked across the Canadian line at Chick-A-Biddy Brook, but United States marshals and Canadian officials broke up the group, captured the officials, and sent the privates home. The movement soon died out.

In 1881 Vermont's Chester A. Arthur became president of the United States, and another Vermonter, Levi P. Morton, was elected vice president in 1888. In 1896 Vermont became the first state ever

The Battle of Manila Bay. *Painting by F.C. Yohn.*

*Painting of
Dewey at Manila.*

to provide for absentee voting by law. The greatest American hero to emerge from the short war with Spain in 1898 was Vermont-born Admiral George Dewey. In 1910 the famous Long Trail for hikers was begun by the Green Mountain Club under the leadership of James P. Taylor.

With unusual foresight, the Vermont legislature appropriated a million dollars in the spring of 1917 for war use. This is especially notable because it was done before the United States entered World War I, placing Vermont in a much better situation than many of the other states to assume wartime responsibilities. During the war, Admiral Henry T. Mayo of Burlington served as commander in chief of the Atlantic fleet. He was the fourth admiral from this inland state to serve his country in a major war. A total of about sixteen thousand Vermont men and women served in this war, and 642 lost their lives.

41

On August 3, 1923, a Vermont man was visiting at the Plymouth home of his father. Suddenly the family was awakened with the startling news that the president of the United States had died, and the Vermont man, until then vice president, was now the country's president. The man was Calvin Coolidge. In the flickering yellow light of the kerosene lamps, Colonel John Coolidge, Calvin's father and a justice of the peace, performed a ceremony that has been called "a dramatic event, unparalleled in American annals."

At 2:47 A.M. Calvin Coolidge and his father stood beside a simple table in the house. The son placed his hand on the family's much-worn Bible, while the father solemnly administered the oath of office to the nation's new president. According to the Vermont Board of Historic Sites, "Never before or since has a president taken the oath of office from his own father, in his own home, and under such unique surroundings. This stirring event will always occupy not only an indelibly important niche in American history, but it holds an appeal, in its uniqueness and moving simplicity, to all Americans."

Calvin Coolidge (right) succeeded to the presidency when President Warren G. Harding died in 1923.

In late 1927 Vermont suffered the worst flood in the history of the state. Large portions of several communities were washed away. Long stretches of many roads and railroads vanished and at least sixty people lost their lives. At Montpelier raging floodwaters stormed through the streets, reaching second-floor windows in many places, and the city was isolated from the rest of the nation. A program of dams and flood controls has since helped stop such disastrous flooding.

On August 27, 1929, the opening of the Lake Champlain Bridge at Chimney Point provided the first span across the lake. The cost was shared by New York and Vermont.

Prior to World War II Vermont maintained its reputation for foresight in its preparation for war. Newspaper columnist Charles Rice relates of Vermont: "In 1941, the good people of that state got so enraged at the Nazis that they declared war on Germany two months before America did. The declaration was duly voted in the state legislature." During the war 49,942 persons saw service from Vermont, and 1,233 were killed. Among the nation's heroes of that war was the Reverend George Lansing Fox, who left his Gilman parish to serve as a chaplain. Lieutenant Fox and three other chaplains on the ship *Dorchester* sacrificed their lives so that others of the crew might have a chance to live. The brave and unselfish Gilman minister gave his life jacket to a soldier and went down with the ship.

In 1957, completion of the Moore Dam on the Connecticut River brought to the area the largest hydroelectric power development in all of New England as well as a new 3,500-acre (1,416-hectare) lake 11 miles (17.7 kilometers) long, which added large-scale fishing, swimming, and boating resources to the region.

The elections of 1962 brought a striking change in politics. Since the Republican party was founded in the 1850s, Vermont had never elected a Democratic governor until Philip H. Hoff in 1962. Even more startling, Vermont voted Democratic for President Lyndon B. Johnson in 1964. Since Jacob M. Howard, born in Shaftsbury, became one of the founders of the Repbulican party 110 years before, Vermont had always supported the Republican standard-bearer.

In 1974 the state elected Patrick J. Leahy as the first Democratic United States senator in its history. However, the elections of 1976 reversed the trend; Vermonters gave their presidential vote to Gerald Ford and chose Republicans Richard A. Snelling as governor and R.T. Stafford as United States senator.

THE PEOPLE OF VERMONT

Some observers feel that Vermont's vote in national elections is a good indication of the independent character of the people. In 1912 only Utah and Vermont gave their vote to President William Howard Taft. Only two states, Maine and Vermont, voted for Alfred M. Landon against President Franklin D. Roosevelt in 1936.

Vermonters have been called "stubborn as their granite and marble mountains." Probably a better word is "determined." Just as the grim granite mountains are softened by forest greens and brightened by the brilliant colors of autumn, so also is the stern character of the people softened and tempered by concern for the individual and his or her welfare, no matter how ruggedly individualistic all may be.

Innumerable fascinating stories illustrate the rugged independence of the Vermonter. In 1787 the first permanent settler in Montpelier, Colonel Jacob Davis, was snowbound in Brookfield. His children, a boy of fifteen and two younger sisters, were marooned alone in their Montpelier cabin for three months. Upon his return he found the children well and unharmed.

Another story of courage is that of Mrs. Amos Story. Her husband had settled at Salisbury, but before he could send for his wife and small children he was killed by a falling tree. In spite of this, the family came to his claim and stayed there during the American Revolution when most of the other settlers fled. Although her home was burned by Indian raiders, the dauntless pioneer woman soon was able to rebuild it. The Story home was often a welcome haven for the Green Mountain Boys.

Working together, Vermont neighbors could complete even the hardest tasks. On such large jobs as moving a house or barn, the people for miles around would gather with their draft animals for a "drawing bee." As many as thirty yoke of oxen might be used to draw the building across country on skids. When the job was done, the grateful owner would spread a bounteous meal for his neighbors.

Vermonters are a unique breed. As many as twelve hundred contestants might gather at Bethel for tournaments of collar and elbow wrestling, a strenuous individual sport which originated in Vermont. Sometimes a visitor to the state will make the mistake of asking a Vermonter why it seems that cows outnumber people. The answer is likely to be "We prefer 'em." When Governor Wentworth of New Hampshire gave the grant of Guilford in the colonial days, he asked for five hundred acres (about two hundred hectares) to be reserved for him. With tongue in cheek the people set aside the rugged top of the only peak in the neighborhood and called it Governor's Mountain, the name it still bears.

One of Vermont's most extraordinary legends provides another illustration of the willingness of most people to believe that Vermonters are unique. The tale persists that aged Vermont residents were given a drug and then quick-frozen for the winter. In this way they were preserved through the winter at a considerable saving of food and revived, rested and refreshed, in the spring. The story was almost believed by some people, and it was not until 1952 that the origin of the legend was traced to Allen Morse, a storyteller of Calais, Vermont.

Many other nationalities have been added to the original English strains of Vermont. Scottish and Italian stoneworkers came to work the marble and granite quarries and provide the fine skills of stone carving. The Irish arrived in even larger numbers; they started as laborers and advanced rapidly to some of the highest positions in the state. Smaller numbers of Polish, Czech, Russian, Swedish, Welsh, and Austrian descendants also have come to the state. Since the Civil War the largest group of immigrants have been the French Canadians.

Regardless of their origin, most of the people of Vermont take on at least some of the individualistic characteristics of their neighbors.

Among the natural treasures of Vermont are geese (above); deer (below); and trees (right), which cover a large portion of the state and are especially beautiful during the fall.

Natural Treasures

The beautiful and useful sugar maple tree is found only in North America. Probably no other natural treasure is so characteristic of Vermont as the millions of these trees that shade the countryside. A little-known fact about these maples is that the sugar in their sap, which is so much desired for eating, is the very chemical that is also responsible for turning the leaves to their flaming red glory in autumn.

White pine has long been the most important timber tree; there are fourteen other conifers (commonly known as evergreens), as well as oak, hickory, butternut, cherry, birch, elm, beech, ash, and others. Although the forests of Vermont have been used for centuries, 4,250,000 acres (almost 172,000 hectares) are still covered by forest. The three-hundred-year-old pine near Arlington is thought to be the one that now appears on the state seal. The legend is told that a British officer, a guest at Chittenden House, engraved the view he could see from his window (including the tree) on a horn drinking cup. Later, the story goes, this scene was transferred to the state seal, designed in 1779.

The smaller flora of the state are greatly varied. Rare Alpine flowers, similar to those of the Arctic regions, are found on the slopes of Mount Mansfield and at other high elevations. Arbutus, trillium, anemones, ferns, and bloodroot add color to the spring landscape. Surprisingly, forty-three different types of orchids are known in Vermont, along with eighty species of the rose family. The sturdy stalks of the red clover stand large and tall as befits Vermont's state flower.

Most of the larger animals of Vermont were almost exterminated by hunters at an early date. By the 1870s deer were said to be nearly extinct in the state. The last mountain lion (generally known in Vermont as panther or catamount) was killed in 1881. Now protected, moose are seen occasionally in northern areas.

Because of reintroduction and careful conservation in recent years, some of these animals have made spectacular comebacks. Animal lovers purchased seventeen deer in 1878, and hunting of deer was forbidden until 1896. Today, in spite of the fact that hunters kill record numbers of white-tailed deer each hunting season, the number of these animals in Vermont continues to increase. Deer can be taken by bow-and-arrow during sixteen days preceding the regular hunting season. Bears were favorite targets for Vermont hunters even before two Scots of Barnet met a bear in a hand-to-hand fight and clubbed it to death in 1776.

Duck, grouse, and other fowl are popular hunting targets in Vermont. Popular songbirds include the hermit thrush—the much-admired state bird—the brilliant cardinal, and the beautiful, distinctively marked Baltimore oriole.

The Batten Kill in southern Vermont is one of the finest trout streams in the East. More than a dozen varieties of the most popular inland sporting fish, from pike and pickerel to landlocked salmon and smallmouth bass, are found in Vermont. Lake Champlain, along its 120-mile (193-kilometer) Vermont border, is perhaps best known for its mighty sturgeon.

Mineral deposits rank among the most important resources of the state. Some estimates place the depth of Vermont's granite deposits at thirty miles (forty-eight kilometers). The Granite Hills provide an entire mountain range of this important stone, while the supplies of widely varying types of marble seem almost inexhaustible. In the Red Rock Hills is found the so-called Mallett's Bay marble, which is actually dolomite, and other building stone of red color. Talc and asbestos are found along the eastern edges of the Green Mountains. Various clays, such as the kaolin at Monkton, are also important.

People Use Their Treasures

TWO NAMED MORGAN

In Vermont if you speak of Justin Morgan, no one will be sure whether you mean a man or a horse, for both had the same name.

In 1791 a schoolteacher of Randolph Center named Justin Morgan took a two-year-old dark-colored bay stallion as payment for a debt. Full-grown, the horse stood about fourteen hands high and weighed not less than 950 pounds (430 kilograms). "His back and legs were short and heavily muscled . . . his chest deep and wide. His thickly muscled neck was set high on his shoulders. The vigor of his constitution and temperament was evident in his every movement. He was a proud horse with great presence, courage, and endurance, tho' perfectly gentle and kind to handle."

His many fine characteristics made him an extraordinarily valuable horse. It was found that his many sons and daughters and grandsons and granddaughters all had inherited most of his characteristics. The horse came to be known as Justin Morgan in honor of his owner, and the Morgan horse became the first and one of the finest breeds of horses ever to originate in America. They are easily identified by their distinctive conformation. Traditionally, the Morgan horse could outdraw, outrun, and outtrot all other horses. Within fifty years, Morgan horses were found in every state. From the Morgan breed also came several other breeds—American Saddlebred, Standardbred, and the Tennessee Walking Horse.

According to the Vermont Development Department: "No other horse of any breed has so strikingly stamped his own type upon his descendants. The heritage of Morgans is rich in qualities which are so sought after in horses today: sound conformation, good disposition, style and beauty, distinctive breed characteristics, and the ability to perform correctly whatever the task to be done. It seems fitting then that the Morgan Horse with his remarkable characteristics was named the state animal of Vermont in 1961.

"Justin Morgan died in 1821 at the age of 32 years from an untended injury inflicted by another horse. Before that injury he was

The Morgan horse (right) became the first and one of the finest breeds of horses to originate in America.

perfectly sound and free of any blemish. Persons who saw him in 1819 and 1820 described his appearance as 'remarkably pert and youthful.' Age and years of hard labor had not quenched his remarkable spirit or spoiled his temperament."

"SAP'S A RUNNIN'!"

Since the days when the Indians first showed the early settlers that there was "sweet food in trees," nothing has been so typical of Vermont as the cry, "Sap's a runnin'!" One of the greatest joys of childhood from earliest times to the present has been "sugar-on-snow"—the delightful practice of pouring a dipper of pure boiling syrup on pure white snow. It solidifies immediately into Nature's pure candy.

Today Vermont ranks either first or second in maple syrup production every year, tapping more than three million sugar maple trees. Each tree will yield up to 1 gallon (3.8 liters) of sap; 35 gallons

50

(132 liters) of sap are required to make 1 gallon (3.8 liters) of maple syrup. The annual production of maple syrup in Vermont has been running about 400,000 gallons (more than 1,500,000 liters).

A grove of maples is known as a "sugar bush." Here the trees may be eighty feet (twenty-four meters) tall. Trees are seldom ready to produce sugar until they are about forty years old or ten inches (twenty-five centimeters) in diameter. One sugar maker reported that he cut a tree with ring marks indicating an age of more than two hundred years. It bore the marks of tapping one hundred years—the gashes made by the Indians and the holes bored by increasingly good cutting tools, down to the present day.

This "sugar house" in the Green Mountains is used for boiling off maple sap.

Buckets hung on spouts that are placed in maple trees hold the sap.

In Vermont, sugar making may begin as early as February 22 and continue as late as the last week in April. The sap runs only when the temperature is exactly right, and sap runs will be good or poor depending on the weather. In freezing weather no sap flows, nor will it flow when the weather becomes continuously warm. Alternating warm days and cold nights produce the best sap flow. Slanting holes are drilled in each tree. A spout is placed in each of these holes and buckets are hung on the spouts to hold the sap. In large operations plastic tubing now is attached to each spout; the tubes lead to covered central gathering tanks, and then to storage tanks. From the storage tanks the sap runs through evaporators where heat draws off the water and leaves the thicker syrup. Sugar content and flavor vary widely from tree to tree and orchard to orchard, and also from season to season in the same orchard. The quality of Vermont maple syrup is carefully controlled by law.

THEIR BUSINESS IS MONUMENTAL

In 1785 the first marble deposits in the United States were found at East Dorset, and the first commercial marble quarry in the country opened there. For many years, Vermont has been a leader in the production of marble.

The small marble industry was tranformed after the Civil War by Colonel Redfield Proctor of Rutland. His energetic methods brought marble into the field of big business and made his Vermont Marble

52

Company the largest in the country, now with quarries also in Georgia, Alaska, Colorado, and Montana as well as Italy. The headquarters of the company at Proctor have been called the "center of the marble world." Most of the public buildings and even many of Proctor's sidewalks are made of gleaming marble. Among other honors and positions, Colonel Proctor held the post of governor of Vermont.

The quarries at Danby have been used to construct some of the nation's most distinctive buildings, including the magnificent Supreme Court Building in Washington D.C. The Lincoln Memorial and portions of the Capitol Building are also constructed of Vermont marble. The Danby quarries are among the few that are underground. In many places the open cuts of the Vermont quarries have created large man-made canyons. Among the world's most distinctive marbles are those of Isle La Motte—noted for their unusual colors. The famous blue marble quarry at Dorset was reopened in 1963 after being out of operation for a period.

There is so much granite in Vermont that some farms even have the unusual luxury of granite fence corner posts. The Rock of Ages Company at Barre operates the world's largest granite quarries and the world's largest granite-finishing plant. Granite is extremely hard, so cutting and finishing it is difficult. Barre is known as the "world's granite center," comparable to Proctor in marble.

About 90 percent of all the asbestos mined in the United States comes from the Vermont Asbestos Company operations near Lowell. Talc, limestone, and slate are other important mineral products of Vermont. In the Fair Haven region is found the only slate in the country that does not fade in its green, purple, and mottled forms. Total mineral production in Vermont is valued at approximately $40 million.

In earlier times Vermont led in other minerals. At the time of the War of 1812, Vergennes was the largest iron center in the country, producing two tons of cannonballs every day. The first copper mine in the United States was operated at Strafford, and it remained open until 1957. In 1870, Vershire had the largest copper mine in the United States. However, copper deposits have decreased.

VERY CLEVER, THOSE VERMONTERS

Although Vermont does not have any huge manufacturing concerns, the state has played a leading part in many highly specialized industries. This outstanding position was due in large part to the unusual number of inventors and innovators of the state.

Thomas Davenport, born in Williamstown, provided one of the most important and widely used inventions in the world's history. He began with a horseshoe magnet. For what we know today as the "winding" he used strips of silk from his wife's wedding dress. To this magnet he applied a crude armature and produced the first electric motor. His early model provided enough power to run his sawmill for a time as an experiment. Davenport went on to make the first model of an electrically driven automobile. Although he devoted most of his life to mechanics and science and even patented his motor in 1837, he died a poor man, with almost no recognition.

Strangely, Wareham Chase, born in Calais, created an electric motor only two years after Davenport, without any knowledge of Davenport's earlier work. Chase was self-educated and during the almost one hundred years of his life it was said that he never ventured more than thirty miles from his birthplace. The president of General Electric Company examined the Chase motor in 1922 and said it was more finished than that of Davenport. How Chase managed such an accomplishment has never been explained satisfactorily.

Probably the best-known Vermont inventor was Thaddeus Fairbanks, whose name went around the world on the nameplate of his much-used invention. In 1830 Fairbanks patented his first lever platform scale and began its manufacture at St. Johnsbury. He began his experiments to find a means of weighing hemp in a factory; his fortune grew out of the production of every type of scale, from those that weigh pinches of chemicals to vast mechanisms registering the weight of a full freight car.

Asahel Hubbard invented a hydraulic pump at Windsor, and pumps of this type are still being made today. His nephew, George Hubbard, was the inventor of a device found in almost every home—the coffee percolator. Later he turned to another device for the home—an entirely new type of patented glazier's point and an inserter for the points. This completely updated the setting of glass panes in windows.

Nicanor Kendall, son-in-law of Asahel Hubbard, was a gunsmith. After he had accidentally shot himself through the hand, he invented the much safer underhammer rifle. Kendall and his father-in-law manufactured this weapon, and one of their first large orders was from the Republic of Texas. Another Windsor inventor was Richard Smith Lawrence, who later moved to Connecticut and helped to found the Winchester Repeating Arms Company.

The very first patent—patent number one—issued by the United States Patent Office in 1790 went to a Vermont man, Samuel Hopkins. This was for a method of making pearl ash, used in the manufacture of soap.

Other Vermont inventors include Silas Herring, the burglar-proof safe; Silas Hawes, of Shaftsbury, the carpenter's square; and Julio T. Buel. Buel was fishing in a boat one afternoon when one of his mother's silver teaspoons dropped overboard. When he saw a large fish strike at the spoon, Buel went home, borrowed another teaspoon, and fashioned from it the fishing spoon that many fishermen use today.

A.W. Gray devised and manufactured a horsepower machine at Middleton Springs. This was actually operated by horses on a treadmill. After experimenting for eleven years, James Wilson of Bradford produced the first geographical globes manufactured in this country. Isaac Markham was especially important to the stonecutting industry. He rediscovered the lost methods of sawing marble that had been known to the ancient Egyptians.

Springfield has long been known as the "cradle of inventors." These included James Hartness, Amasa Woolson, Adna Brown, Fred Lovejoy, W. Leroy Bryant, E.R. Fellows, and Ralph E. Flanders. Much work was done in Springfield to improve the machine-tool industry. Mainly as a result of this inspired effort, Springfield developed into America's fourth largest machine-tool center, an extraordinary record for a city of only about ten thousand persons.

Perhaps because of the inventiveness of its people, Vermont now can boast of some of the most modern and progressive manufacturing plants in the nation. Roland Vautour, former commissioner of the Vermont Development Department, said, "We're in the space age industry up to our ears. There is a company in western Vermont that manufactures guidance systems for many of America's orbital flights. Reentry vehicles are being manufactured in Burlington as well as all of the relays for the entire Intercontinental Ballistic Missile complex. Memory cores and electroencephalographs are further examples of the diversified and contemporary industries located in Vermont."

Manufacturing in the state has a total value of about $750 million per year.

AGRICULTURE

The dairy industry of Vermont accounts for about 75 percent of the total income from agriculture.

The important Holstein-Frisian Association has its national headquarters at Brattleboro.

Potatoes, corn, apples, and Christmas trees are important crops. A promising new product in the apple industry has been developed in the state. This is red apple syrup, a tasty topping for waffles, pancakes, sundaes, and other delights. David Millington of Shaftsbury was responsible for an earlier development, the wax tree-graft method, that proved important to apple growers and other orchardists.

A small but interesting agricultural industry is the harvesting of commercial ferns, centered in Danby and Chittenden. These are sold to florist wholesalers. Far more important to the Vermont economy, farmers of the state produce a million tons (900,000 metric tons) of hay, which helps to feed the almost four hundred thousand head of cattle and other livestock.

A highlight of Vermont livestock history occurred in 1811 when merino sheep were first brought in from Spain, where they had been carefully guarded. The quality and length of wool fiber from these sheep were a great improvement over those raised before that time in America. The sheep boom continued in Vermont for more than fifty years. In the 1860s the sheep population had grown until there were six sheep for every person in Vermont. Then the market fell off, and the sheep boom ended.

Yearly income from agriculture totals about a quarter of a billion dollars.

TRANSPORTATION AND COMMUNICATION

Fourteen years before Robert Fulton's success, Captain Samuel Morey invented a steamboat. He chugged along the Connecticut River in 1793 in a small boat scarcely large enough to hold the cumbersome, clanking, boiler machinery and firewood to keep it stoked, while the paddle wheels energetically churned the waters. He is said to have patented his work and showed it to Robert Fulton who bought it, giving Morey $100,000 of worthless stock. Morey, disgusted, probably sank his invention in Lake Morey, which bears his name. In 1826, Morey patented an internal combustion engine—a forerunner of the present gasoline engine.

The world's second commercial steamboat operation began in 1808 on Lake Champlain. The Champlain Transportation Company, with headquarters at Burlington, began operating on the lake in 1828.

Another dramatic transportation development in Vermont was the opening of the country's first canal in 1802. This canal, at Bellows Falls, was constructed to permit boats to bypass the falls. It made the Connecticut River navigable from Wells River to Long Island Sound. The old dream of water transportation from Lake Champlain to the Hudson River was realized with the opening of the Champlain Canal in 1823. This gave New York City a more direct link with Montreal.

There are nearly 14,000 miles (about 22,500 kilometers) of roads and highways in Vermont today. This is a far cry from the first road in the state—the old Crown Point military road. Modern limited-access federal interstate highways in Vermont now total more than 300 miles (480 kilometers).

The Vermont Central Railroad, first in the state, broke ground at Northfield in 1846. There was a great celebration on December 18, 1849, when the Rutland Railroad became the first road into Burlington from Boston. Trains from Burlington and Boston met at Summit; there were flags and bunting, shouts and speechmaking, and waters from Lake Champlain and Boston Harbor were poured together.

The claim is made that Alvin Adams founded the nation's first express line when he went into the business between Windsor and Woodstock. This developed into the Adams Express Company, a competitor of Wells Fargo. The company still operates as a leading financial institution, with headquarters in New York.

One of the most unusual enterprises in the history of journalism was carried on in Vermont by James Johns of Huntington. In 1834, Johns began the Vermont *Autograph and Remarker.* Every copy of every issue of this newspaper was pen-printed by hand by Johns himself for the incredible period of forty years until his death in 1874. Some files of this unique paper are kept in the Vermont Historical Society.

The *Rutland Herald,* established in 1794, is the oldest newspaper still operating in the state. The *Burlington Free Press,* begun in 1848, is the oldest daily.

An interesting event in Vermont's publishing history was the Vermont Bible, published at Windsor in 1812. This was illustrated with woodcuts by Isaac Eddy of Weathersfield, which were crude but are highly valued by collectors today. Another notable event was the establishment of a newspaper, *The Journal of the Times,* at Bennington by William Lloyd Garrison, who later became a renowned newspaperman and abolitionist. Woodstock produced the first Greek lexicon printed in the America.

Shunpiking Vermonters as well as out-of-state tourists enjoy taking the back roads in this lovely state.

The birthplace of Calvin Coolidge in Plymouth.

60

Human Treasures

One of Vermont's greatest distinctions is the large number of its people who have gained fame for worthwhile accomplishments. According to some records, there have been more Vermont natives listed in *Who's Who in America* than from any other state in proportion to population.

MR. PRESIDENT

The only native-born Vermonter to become president in his own right was Calvin Coolidge, who was born back of the family store and post office in Plymouth on the fourth of July 1872. He gained fame as governor of Massachusetts and was elected vice president under Warren Harding. His life in this post was described by renowned journalist William Allen White: "So Coolidge, silently dining and meekly clowning his quiet way through official Washington society by night and watching the Senate by day with no responsibilities, no anxieties, except to send a part of his paycheck every month back to his Northampton bank to watch the $25,000 grow—symbolizing the doctrine, work and save—he was, as it were, politically embalmed."

As the thirtieth president of the United States, Coolidge pleased many and disappointed others, who complained that "he didn't do anything." President Coolidge strongly felt that the president and the government should interfere as little as possible in the lives of the people, and his policies carried out that belief. There appears to be a growing feeling that many historians have treated President Coolidge and his administration more harshly than was deserved and that his abilities were much greater than is recognized.

In any event, with the slogan "Keep Cool with Coolidge," Silent Cal, as he was commonly called, was elected to a full four-year term in 1924. With his plain rural background, Mr. Coolidge was the first "man of the people" to become president in several generations. The great prosperity that the country enjoyed during his administration gave him immense popularity throughout his term. When he announced in a simple, one-sentence declaration, "I do not choose to run for president in 1928," many were stunned.

The highly respected Mrs. Coolidge was also a Vermont native, born Grace Anne Goodhue, at Burlington. She was a graduate of the University of Vermont. President Coolidge died in 1933 and his wife in 1957.

Chester Alan Arthur was born at Fairfield, October 5, 1830. He was an early supporter of civil rights, and as a New York attorney persuaded the courts to rule that slaves who were transported through New York automatically became free. He was also responsible for a ruling that blacks on New York streetcars must be given the same treatment as other persons. Behind-the-scenes moves at the Republican national convention in 1880 saw him placed on the ticket as vice president under James Garfield. When Garfield was assassinated in 1881, Arthur became the twenty-first president.

With unique generosity, President Arthur donated all his salary as president to Garfield's widow. Arthur influenced the passage of the Pendleton Civil Service Act in 1883 and began the civil service program. He also initiated the rebuilding of the then-obsolete United States Navy. His party refused to nominate him in 1884 but he unselfishly supported James G. Blaine, the Republican candidate. President Arthur died in 1886 and is buried at Albany, New York.

As young men both Presidents Garfield and Arthur taught, at different times, in Oak Grove Seminary at Pownal.

THE ROBIN HOODS OF VERMONT

Ethan Allen has been described as "an able, self-taught, self-made man with an arrogant swagger." With his brothers, he operated the Onion River Company, selling land around Winooski. Leading his Green Mountain Boys, Allen gained something of the reputation of an American Robin Hood—a well-meaning fellow who robbed the rich of their ill-gotten lands and protected the interests of the poor, although all this was done outside the actual letter of any law.

After his brilliant capture of Fort Ticonderoga the famous story is told that Allen paid one of his rare visits to church at Bennington. After a long prayer in which Parson Jedediah Dewey gave most of the credit for the victory to the Almighty, Allen interrupted the service to say in a mocking way, "Parson Dewey, please make mention of my being there, too." This may have been Allen's revenge for an earlier service when he had taken exception to one of the preacher's remarks and started to leave. When the parson pointed a finger at his parishioner and shouted, "Sit down, thou blasphemer, and listen to the Word of God!" Allen meekly sat down.

Not long after the capture of Fort Ticonderoga, Allen led an unsuccessful attack on Montreal in Canada and was captured. He spent three years in an English prison. Much to his regret he missed the Battles of Hubbardton and Bennington, but another respected Green Mountain Boy, Seth Warner, played a key role in those struggles.

In *A Narrative of Ethan Allen's Captivity,* Allen revealed his many exploits of daring, such as his leap through a window of the Richards' house at Bridgeport to escape six pursuing British soldiers. His other book, *Reason the Only Oracle of Man,* gave him the reputation of being "one of the most Godless men in America," and he was called by some the Anti-Christ of Vermont.

In his later years, Allen lived in Burlington in the style of a lord of the manor. When he died in 1789, the president of Yale University, Ezra Stiles, wrote in his diary: "Feb. 13—Genl. Ethan Allen of Vermont died & went to hell this day." Today time has mellowed the opinions held about Ethan Allen, and he is usually ranked high among those who contributed to freedom's cause.

Of the other Allen brothers, Ira was the most outstanding. He was considered more brilliant than Ethan. Ira Allen was especially important in preparing the Vermont constitution of 1777. He served as treasurer and surveyor-general of the republic of Vermont and wrote a "free-thinking" book called *Oracles of Reason.* He died penniless, but his wife had previously been given the town of Irasburg, named in Ira Allen's honor, so she and the family were able to carry on. Another Allen brother, Levi, was a Tory.

IN THE PUBLIC EYE

In addition to its presidents, Vermont has contributed a long procession of notable men in public life. Levi P. Morton, born at Shoreham, was vice president under Benjamin Harrison. Morton was also governor of New York. The Little Giant, Stephen A. Douglas, was born at Brandon. When he left for Illinois to begin his great career, he had only thirty-seven cents in his pocket. Another leader in the mid-nineteenth century was Thaddeus Stevens, born at Danville, probably the most influential man in America after the Civil War. Senator Justin S. Morrill's work is described later in this book.

Among governors of the state, the first, Thomas Chittenden, was interesting. A towering figure with only one eye and without formal education, he governed Vermont for eighteen years. Governor Isaac Tichenor held his post for eleven years; he also had a noteworthy career as a Federalist leader in Washington. One story is that while dining at his Bennington home with friends, he saw a game bird in the tree outside, called for his gun, and shot the bird through the window without rising from the table. A later governor, James Hartness, was a leading figure in amateur astronomy. He also pioneered in aviation. At the age of fifty-five he made his first solo flight and received the first pilot's license issued in Vermont.

The most famous leaders of the Mormon faith were born in Vermont. Joseph Smith, founder of the movement, was born on a remote farm between Royalton and Sharon. Brigham Young, who created the Mormon settlement in Utah out of the wilderness, was born at Whitingham, son of a poor basket maker.

A well-known Vermont native became the first United States ambassador to the United Nations. This was Warren Austin, native of Highgate.

Vermont's outstanding military leader of the modern period is George Dewey, born at Montpelier. In 1897, when war with Spain appeared near, Commodore Dewey was appointed to head the American fleet in Asia, although several other officers had seniority for the post. When he heard that war had been declared, Dewey sailed his fleet 600 miles (965 kilometers) at full speed. On his flagship *Olympia,* at the head of his fleet, Dewey steamed into Manila Bay in the Philippines and calmly gave a command to the captain of the *Olympia:* "You may fire when you are ready, Gridley." That fire was so deadly that all of the Spanish ships in the bay were knocked out, including the Spanish flagship *Reina Cristina.* No American lives were lost in this naval battle. Almost overnight, Commodore Dewey became the great American hero. The parade given in his honor in Washington was the greatest ever given an American up to that time, and other cities matched the enthusiasm. Congress created for him a new rank—Admiral of the Navy.

Another Vermont hero of the Spanish-American War was Captain Charles Clark, born in Bradford. His battleship *Oregon,* the pride of the navy, was in San Francisco when he was ordered to Santiago, Cuba. The ship sped down the west coast of the Americas and plunged through the Strait of Magellan. This had never been navigated before by a modern battleship. When he reached Santiago after 15,000 miles (24,000 kilometers) and a record sixty-six days of travel, Captain Clark and his ship had achieved a noteworthy advancement of modern warfare. He also had helped prove the need for a canal in Central America.

CREATIVE VERMONTERS

Some of Vermont's most famous writers were adopted sons and daughters. English writer Rudyard Kipling married Caroline Balestier of Brattleboro in 1892. They lived at Dummerston for almost four years. Kipling wrote a few of his best-known works while in Vermont, including the two *Jungle Books, Captains Courageous, The Seven Seas,* and *The Day's Work.* He did not endear himself to the people around him and in his autobiography he wrote,"so they watched as secretively as the New England or British peasant can, and what toleration they extended to the 'Britisher' was solely for the sake of 'the Balestier girl.' "

Another adopted Vermonter of great fame was Robert Frost, for many years poet laureate of the state. Part of his love for Vermont may be explained by the quotation from his work placed on the marker outside his home near Ripton:

Breathes there a bard who isn't moved
When he finds his verse is understood
And not entirely disapproved
By his Country and his Neighborhood?

Poet Eugene Field was brought up in Newfane; Sinclair Lewis and Dorothy Thompson made their home at Barnard. Much of the work of Dorothy Canfield Fisher of Arlington had to do with Vermont, and she was much loved in the state because of her interest in the state and its people. Critic Alexander Woollcott and actor Harpo Marx called themselves the Summer Green Mountain Boys.

Royall Tyler of Guilford has been called Vermont's earliest man of letters. He wrote the first American drama performed in this country (1787), a comedy called *The Contrast.* His novel *The Algerine Captive* is said to have "presented the first native American types in our literature." He was chief justice of the Vermont Supreme Court for nine years.

Rowland E. Robinson, born on a Vermont farm, probably re-created best the speech, manners, and customs of the people of Vermont. Poet Charles Gamage Eastman is sometimes known as the Burns of New England. Henry Norman Hudson, a Shakespeare critic, edited the twenty-volume *Harvard Shakespeare,* still used by many students and scholars. Historian Zadock Thompson, born in Bridgewater, paid his way through the University of Vermont by publishing an annual almanac. When the printer reminded him once that he had forgotten his forecast for part of July, he quickly said the unlikely words, "Snow about this time." When it actually did snow in July of that year, he gained a great reputation as a prophet.

Possibly most unusual of all Vermont literary persons was T.P. James, described as a "tramp printer," who finished Dickens' *The Mystery of Edwin Drood* in such a professional way that it astonished many experts. He claimed to have done this by putting himself into a trance whenever he wrote.

Vermont artists include Thomas Waterman Wood of Montpelier and Hiram Powers, born near Woodstock, a famous American sculptor of his time. On New Year's Eve in 1856, Larkin Mead, a store clerk of Brattleboro, fashioned an angel from snow and ice at Linden and Main streets in Brattleboro. Because of the cold, the figure lasted several days, and many people, including reporters from Boston, came to see the beautiful work. His Snow Angel helped bring him later fame. His largest work is the Lincoln Memorial at Springfield, Illinois. Mead's younger brother, William Rutherford, was a prominent architect and president of the American Academy in Rome.

Another popular Vermont architect was Richard Morris Hunt. His brother, artist William Morris Hunt, encouraged the French painter Jean Francis Millet at a time when the French critics were making fun of his work.

The highlands of Vermont are celebrated by Arlington composer Carl Ruggles in his symphonic work, *Marching Mountains.*

SUCH INTERESTING PEOPLE

Among the heroes of the American Revolution were Richard Wallace of Thetford and Ephraim Webster of Newbury. Swimming in the icy waters of Lake Champlain with their clothes tied to their heads, they slipped past the British warships to carry important messages to the other side.

Another war hero was Major Benjamin Whitcomb. He slipped into Canada alone, declaring that he would kill a British general. He managed to find a general riding in his carriage, shot and killed him, and escaped unharmed through the enemy country.

Prominent women of Vermont include Henrietta (Hetty) Howland Robinson Green, known as the richest woman in America, and also renowned for her eccentric ways. Fanny Kilgore, born in Craftsbury, became the first woman attorney to practice in the United States. A Vermont heroine of the American Revolution was Ann Story of Salisbury.

"Jubilee" Jim Fisk, railroad tycoon, stock market plunger, and celebrated playboy, was born in Pownal. For some time he kept his headquarters in Brattleboro. Another Vermont-born tycoon was H.A.W. Tabor, who made his fortune in Colorado mining. He was a subject of the opera *Baby Doe*. John Deere, implement manufacturer and inventor of the steel plow, was born at Rutland, and Edwin L. Drake, the first to drill a modern oil well, was a native of Castleton. Carroll S. Page at one time operated the largest tannery in the country at Hyde Park; he was nicknamed Calfskin Page after he became the world's largest dealer in calfskins.

One of Vermont's most individualistic millionaires was Joseph Battell of Bread Loaf, who established the Bread Loaf Inn. Mr. Battell hated automobiles, and when guests came, they had to leave their autos on his estate three miles (about five kilometers) from the house, where his servants met them with horses. Each week he published in his newspaper a full page telling of the most horrible auto accidents of the week. He collected "mountains and Morgan horses," and compiled the two-volume *Morgan Horse Register*.

Columbus Smith built an amazing home on his estate. The house was covered with elaborate frescoes, statuary, and Victorian furnishings. He left his estate, including the house, "for the purpose of founding a good and comfortable home for good old Christian women not addicted to drink."

Wilson A. "Snowflake" Bentley of Jericho had an unusual specialty. For forty-five years Bentley photographed snowflakes in his refrigerated camera room and made large prints of them. He became the greatest authority in that field and left fifty-three hundred microphotos of snowflakes.

Edwin James, was the first botanist to study and explore the Rocky Mountains. Another great scholar was George P. Marsh. During his years in Italy he became a friend of King Victor Emmanuel II and was noted as one of the first to call for the conservation of natural resources.

Truman H. Safford of Royalton began his scientific life as a mathematical prodigy. Before he reached his tenth birthday he could perform such mathematical feats as the mental multiplication of two numbers each with eighteen digits. As head of the Harvard Observatory, he later became one of the best-known astronomers.

68

Teaching and Learning

Some of the most prominent leaders and important advances in education have been associated with Vermont.

One of the world's most influential men in education, John Dewey, was born at Burlington in 1859. He was the main developer of what came to be known as Progressive Education. Dewey also has been given much credit as a philosopher. He created a system of thought which is known as Instrumentalism.

An earlier Vermont educator who had a great influence on world education was Samuel Read Hall. In 1823 Hall opened at Concord Center the first normal school, or teacher training institution, in the country. Hall published the first text ever written on how to teach, and among his other accomplishments he developed the blackboard and introduced the first practice teaching.

Justin Smith Morrill, born at Strafford, was important in education not as a teacher but for what he did to improve education. During his more than forty-three years in the United States House and Senate from Vermont, he never lost an election. The Morrill Act, which he wrote, created an entirely new system of education in the United States. It marked the first time the federal government had taken an active part in education. The Morrill Act provided federal lands to the states to support colleges and universities devoted to teaching agriculture, home economics, and other mechanical and social subjects. Senator Morrill may be considered the father of our entire system of federal-state technical education.

One of the first institutions to begin operations under the Morrill Act was the University of Vermont. The Vermont legislature had passed a university act as early as 1791, when a charter was granted and the state gave 29,000 acres (11,740 hectares) of wild forest lands as an endowment. The man most responsible for planning the university at Burlington was Ira Allen. The University of Vermont first opened in 1801. Today it operates colleges of medicine, nursing, education, agriculture, engineering, and liberal arts.

The university supervises the Proctor Maple Research Farm at Underhill and the Morgan Horse Farm at Weybridge. "Champlain," the university's school song, is believed to be the only one that praises only a university's natural setting.

Today fifteen four-year colleges and universities are located within the boundaries of the Green Mountain State.

The nationally respected Middlebury College was chartered in 1800. Middlebury operates the Bread Loaf School of Creative Writing at Ripton. Joseph Battell gave 30,000 acres (12,140 hectares), including his Bread Loaf Inn, to the college, making possible the now world-renowned institution for writers. Widely known writers who have helped to teach Bread Loaf courses have included Robert Frost, resident of Ripton.

Norwich University of Northfield is usually ranked among the outstanding military institutions in the country. Many of the nation's leading military men have been Norwich graduates, including Admiral Dewey.

State colleges operate at Castleton, Johnson, and Lyndonville. Other colleges include Windham College, Putney; Bennington and St. Joseph College, Bennington; St. Michael's College, Winooski Park; Trinity College, Burlington; and Goddard College, Plainfield. Marlboro College in Marlboro is the site of a summer school of music founded by renowned pianist Rudolf Serkin.

An unusual development in education came when Vermont "adopted" Dartmouth College, although it was across the Connecticut River in New Hampshire. New Hampshire had "shown a very cool disposition" toward its own college, and Vermont wanted to keep the nearby institution going. Vermont granted Dartmouth 23,000 acres (9,300 hectares) of Vermont land, which later became the entire township of Wheelock. At that time this was half of Dartmouth's endowment. Much of this land is still owned by Dartmouth. For this act of generosity, Vermont stands as probably the only state that ever gave state aid to an educational institution in another state. Dartmouth still provides scholarships for students from Wheelock.

The first public elementary school in the state was established at Norwich in 1785. By 1826 the idea of statewide education supported by public funds had become established.

70

Springtime view of the University of Vermont at Burlington.

Enchantment of Vermont

"UNSPOILED VERMONT, THE BECKONING COUNTRY"

"Vermont is everyone's second state," said historian Allan Nevins. Famed writer Bernard De Voto expressed the same thought somewhat differently: "There is no more Yankee than Polynesian in me, but whenever I go to Vermont I feel I am traveling toward my home place."

A rapidly increasing number of visitors are discovering their "second state." Recreation now brings much prosperity to Vermont.

The fast growth of the travel business in the state is illustrated by skiing. As recently as 1958 the ski business in Vermont totaled only $14 million. Only six years later, in 1964, the state's ski business had reached $40 million. In the state where the ski tow originated, there are now 60 miles (96 kilometers) of ski tows, carrying one hundred thousand passengers an hour. It is easy to imagine an endless line of colorfully clad people ascending ceaselessly, only to come plunging down the slopes of feathery snow. With its many ski areas, Vermont is the leading ski state of the East, providing the most dependable snow conditions, with as much as 120 feet (36.5 meters) in the Green Mountains.

Outdoor attractions include all other winter sports, especially ice fishing; all water sports, including boating in everything from canoes to yachts on Lake Champlain; trail rides; and hiking. The Long Trail provides 260 miles (418 kilometers) of delightful hiking across the crests of the Green Mountains. There are dozens of state forests and parks.

For visitors, typical Vermont delights include country auctions, arts and crafts, fairs, farm vacations, antiques and early American reproductions, country stores, museums, the joys of back-road tour-

In Vermont, the leading ski state of the East,
two skiers rest before skiing down a mountain.

73

ing or "shunpiking," maple sugar and maple manufacturing plants open to the public, neighborly visits to Canada, and more than a hundred covered bridges. Many of these bridges are the early type made with only ax, adz, and saw.

The unsurpassed scenery of the Green Mountain State is everywhere. Nothing is more beautiful than Vermont in autumn when the ridges blaze with flaming red maples, and every mountainside is enveloped in the most spectacular reds, oranges, and yellows, set off against the emerald background of the evergreens.

Wherever they may be in the state, most visitors will agree with the tourist who said, "Unspoiled Vermont continually beckons to me."

MONTPELIER-BARRE

As the shadows of the surrounding hills sweep across Montpelier at sunset, almost the last remaining bright spot is the symmetrical dome of the beautiful capitol as its pure gold outline captures and reflects the last rays of the sun. The austere but gracious lines of the capitol are said to reflect something of the character of Vermont's people.

This is the third capitol building of Vermont. The first building, of wood, was completed in 1808 with funds contributed by local citizens. The second—largely granite and brick—was completed in 1833. Its interior was destroyed by fire in 1857. The present larger statehouse, dedicated in 1859, is similar to the earlier one. The building houses the sessions of the legislature; the offices of the governor, lieutenant governor, secretary of state, sergeant-at-arms, and legislative draftsman; and the legislative reference bureau. The State Office Building, built in 1947, and State Administration Building in Capitol Square, opened in 1960, house other state offices. Legislative space is provided in an annex to the statehouse (completed in 1886).

Design of the capitol was based on a Greek temple. The main feature of the capitol exterior is what has been called a "magnificent

The capitol building, Montpelier.

portico," supported on granite columns. Granite for the capitol building was hauled from Barre by teams of oxen. Crowning the building is a statue of the harvest goddess, *Ceres,* by Larkin G. Mead. The interior is decorated with marble and ornamental iron. The Senate and House of Representatives chambers are said to be among the most beautiful of all such rooms.

One of the pioneer settlers, Jacob Davis, chose the name of a French town for the infant community. It is taken from the words for mountain (*mont*) and bare (*peller),* meaning a bare mountain. Colonel Davis and other settlers began to clear land for Montpelier in 1787. State Street was cut through fields of nodding corn stalks in 1807, two years after Montpelier was named the capital. Situated on

75

the main pass through the Green Mountains and at the junction of rivers and roads, Montpelier soon became an important trading point. The granite industry has been responsible for much of the city's growth. It is also an insurance center. The National Life Insurance Company, founded by Julius Y. Dewey, father of Montpelier native Admiral George Dewey, has its impressive granite headquarters building in the city. Five other large insurance companies also have headquarters in the city, making Montpelier the third largest insurance center in New England.

The Vermont Historical Society Museum is housed in the granite State Administration Building. Among interesting Vermont relics in the museum are the first world globes made by James Wilson in 1812 and the Nobel Prize medal of Sinclair Lewis. One of the most prized historical exhibits in the country is the Stephen Daye press, first printing press ever to operate in what is now the United States.

In March 1793 two burly men were fighting—punching and wrestling and thrashing around on the barn floor; around them stood their neighbors, each rooting for his favorite. Suddenly one of the men, named Thompson, failed to rise. The other man, the town blacksmith, named Sherman, jumped up and gasped, "There, by God, the name is Barre." And sure enough the name has been Barre (pronounced as in "carry") ever since.

The present city of Barre was at that time named Wildersburgh, but many residents thought the name was not "cultured" enough. They held a town meeting in a local barn to decide between the names Holden, Thompson's home town in Massachusetts, and Barre, Sherman's former home, also in Massachusetts. The vote ended in a tie, and tempers became so hot that Barre's name was finally decided by a fight. One of the first duties of an early Barre doctor was to remove splinters from the barn floor that had buried themselves in the two combatants.

Two of Vermont's most typical museums are located in Barre. One is the John Shelby Maple Museum, containing maple processing demonstrations, murals of sugaring, and antique sugaring equipment. There are even samples on hand for tasting. The Granite Museum shows granite cutters at work and other interesting exhibits on the granite industry. Some of the mammoth granite quarries and carving plants in the area, with their skilled craftsmen, are open to visitors.

In Barre is a unique statue of Robert Burns. This was commissioned by Italian stoneworkers of the area in honor of their co-workers from Scotland. It is considered a particularly fine example of granite carving.

BURLINGTON AND THE NORTHWEST

The largest city in Vermont, Burlington, is known as the Queen City. It was settled in 1773, and the fur trade, as well as its position on Lake Champlain, soon attracted many settlers. In addition to housing industry, Burlington is a university town. At the eastern edge of the city the University of Vermont attracts many visitors with its annual Shakespeare festival in the Robert Hall Fleming Museum of the university, where there are historical, Oriental, and modern art collections.

Ethan Allen Park covers part of the farm of the early Vermont hero. In the park, a memorial tower offers a splendid vista of the lake and rolling mountains. Burlington is the terminal for exciting ferry trips over the gleaming lake.

At nearby Shelburne is one of the nation's outstanding museums, the Shelburne Museum—a forty-acre (sixteen-hectare) reconstruction of American life of the long ago, as well as the more recent past, displayed in more than thirty buildings. The museum is entered through one of Vermont's finest covered bridges, which formerly spanned the Lamoille River at Cambridge. The most spectacular exhibit is the old side-wheeler steamboat *Ticonderoga,* brought overland on specially made tracks. More than two hundred locomotives and historic railroad cars are on display, along with a fascinating collection of cigar store Indians, sleighs, buggies, and other items.

The submerged hulks of some of the ships sunk by Benedict Arnold in the Revolutionary War may still be seen near Panton. The keel and some ribs of Arnold's flagship *Congress* were salvaged and brought to the old Barnes House near Chimney Point, where there is a fascinating collection of old-time objects.

Addison was one of the first settlements of Vermont. To the south, among other distinctions, Bridgeport is known as the birthplace of the famous Morgan racing horse, Black Hawk.

Middlebury has long been a noted educational center. The Female Academy was directed by famed educator Emma Hart Willard, who provided some of America's earliest advanced education for women. Abernethy Library of Middlebury College has an outstanding collection of writings and memorabilia of Robert Frost, Henry David Thoreau, and Walt Whitman. Other interesting collections are housed in the Sheldon Museum of Middlebury. The main barn of the University of Vermont's Morgan Horse Farm near Middlebury has been called "one of the most distinctive structures of its type in the United States."

The profanity of the teamsters who drove their wagons up a steep and muddy slope near Bristol disturbed Joseph Greene. He had the Lord's Prayer carved on a rock near the spot in the hope that it would discourage the swearing. It is unlikely that this effect was achieved but the interesting carving may still be seen.

In 1785 John Broadt was found living as a hermit near present-day Bristol. He had hidden there for twelve years, thinking he had killed a man. When he found the man was alive, he was able to return to his home.

One of the longest ski lifts in the East is the aerial gondola at Sugar Bush Valley Ski Area near Warren. The region around Roxbury is particularly renowned for the brilliance of its autumn coloring.

Waitsfield offers the Bundy Art Gallery, an interesting collection of modern art. At Huntington is John Teal's unique experimental farm, devoted to breeding and studying the musk ox. Visitors to Richmond are especially interested in the old "round" church, which is not round at all but actually has sixteen sides. The breathtaking scenery of Bolton Gorge stretches where the Winooski River has carved its great depths between Waterbury and Bolton.

The Stowe region is renowned as the Ski Capital of the East, where "there's always snow in Stowe." The area is one of the most picturesque in Vermont, and Smuggler's Notch near Stowe is an impressive highway pass.

The peaks of Mount Mansfield make up the mountain's "face." In modern times, the "nose" supports a television transmission antenna. The best view is said to be from the "chin," although the "nose" is almost as good. From Mount Mansfield one can see Mount Royal, which gives the Canadian city Montreal its name.

Brother Joseph Dutton, a native of Stowe, is remembered by a memorial Catholic church near Stowe. Father Dutton joined Father Damien, the leper priest, in his work at the Hawaiian leper colony. Stowe has gained further fame as the home of the Trapp family of singers, known to all through *The Sound of Music.*

The "round" church in Richmond (left) actually has sixteen sides.

There are more than one hundred covered bridges in Vermont.

The opera house at Hyde Park is the headquarters of the Lamoille Players. Montgomery has the unusual and possibly unique distinction of having six covered bridges in the town. A reputation of a different kind belongs to Enosburg Falls, which was once the unofficial national capital of patent medicine manufacturing. Four patent medicine fortunes were made in the small town.

The simple frame house in which President Chester A. Arthur was born near Fairfield has been reproduced there.

The "Heroes" honored in the names of North Hero and South Hero on Grande Isle were the Allens, Ethan (North) and Ira (South). The Hyde Log Cabin, built on the island in 1783, is considered to be the oldest log cabin still standing in the United States.

THE NORTHEAST

The town of Derby Line demonstrates the goodwill between Canada and the United States. Its International Rotary Club and Haskell Library and Opera House are built astride the boundary line between the two nations, and a Canadian village seems to merge with Derby Line. The Haskell Opera House is built so that the audience sits in the United States and the stage is in Canada. The story is told that American officers had to watch helplessly while a fugitive performed on the stage, safe from them by virtue of being out of the country in Canada.

Possibly the most famous native son of Island Pond is entertainer Rudy Vallee.

Lake Willoughby is considered one of the most beautiful lakes in the world; it is often compared to Lake Lucerne in Switzerland.

Newport is Vermont's most northerly city, spread along the hilly shoreline of Lake Memphremagog. It is one of the most popular gateways between New England and Canada. Near Newport Center the Missisquoi River forms a beautiful cascade known as Troy Falls. From Jay Peak near Westfield, it is said that the streets of Montreal can be seen on a clear day. An interesting old stone building erected singlehandedly by the Reverend Alexander Twilight is located in Brownington. He hauled the stones with an ox, squared them himself, brought them up a ramp to the construction area, and in two years had built a 60-by-45-foot (18-by-13.7-meter) building, four stories high, that he used for his academy.

A strange series of events began at what came to be called Runaway Pond near Glover. A group of workers were cutting out a channel so that the pond would drain into the lower Mud Pond and raise its water level. Suddenly the entire north shore of the upper pond started to wash away; with a great roar, the whole lake became a boiling fury, turning into a tremendous whirlpool and then rushing from its bed.

Riders dashed down the valley to warn the residents; the wall of water, sixty feet (eighteen meters) high, swept everything in its path—including mills and great trees. The flood reached Lake

Memphremagog at Newport, twenty-five miles (forty kilometers) away, in just six hours. The pond was completely drained in only ninety minutes, but mud flowed from the bottom for several more hours.

The group known as Holy Rollers originated at Hardwick. Kent's Corner had a large group of another sect known as Millerites. They believed that the world would end on midnight, December 13, 1843. A sizeable congregation gathered at Old West Church in Kent's Corner. As the clock struck the hour, many screamed and some fainted. When nothing happened, the congregation silently filed out.

The three museums of St. Johnsbury are notable cultural achievements for a town of its size. These are the Fairbanks Museum of Natural Science and Planetarium, the Maple Museum, and St. Johnsbury Athenaeum, an unusual library and art gallery. The Fairbanks Museum was presented to St. Johnsbury by Colonel Franklin Fairbanks in 1891. The Fairbanks scale works is still the principal industry of the town, which was named in honor of Ethan Allen's French friend St. John de Crèvecoeur.

One of the most dramatic events in Vermont history occurred in a courtroom at Danville. The notorious international bank robber Bristol Bill, who had defied the lawmen of two continents, was captured in the little town of Groton. As he was being sentenced at Danville, he suddenly shouted in defiance and stabbed the prosecuting attorney to death in the presence of the judge and spectators.

East Corinth is probably the most photographed village in New England. Pictures of this quiet hamlet are used when advertisers or editors want to show a typical New England village.

Brookfield is noted for its floating bridge over Mirror Lake; it is held up by almost four hundred oak barrels and will support a ten-ton load (nine metric tons).

The Tunbridge Fair, begun in 1867, is an annual affair. It is one of the outstanding town fairs in the country, and is nicknamed the Tunbridge Little World's Fair. One of its distinctive features is the demonstration of many old handicrafts—pressing cheese by hand; dipping candles; and carding, spinning, dyeing, and weaving wool. The carnival spirit of the fair is unusual in New England.

SOUTHERN VERMONT

The Brattleboro slogan "Where Vermont begins" could just as well read "Where Vermont began." Two miles (3.2 kilometers) to the south of the present town was old Fort Dummer, first permanent European settlement in Vermont. The son of Captain Timothy Dwight of the Fort was the first settler's child born in Vermont.

Jacob Estey gained control of an organ manufacturing company at Brattleboro in 1855 and built up a large organ business. At one time the town was the world center of organ manufacturing, with both the Estey and Minshall organ factories. The Retreat at Brattleboro is claimed to be the country's largest private mental institution. Speculator-playboy Jim Fisk is buried in Brattleboro's Prospect Hill cemetery.

At Guilford is the grave of Vermont pioneer Benjamin Carpenter. The inscription on his tombstone reads: "Left this world and 146 persons of lineal posterity, March 29, 1804, aged 78 years, 10 months and 12 days, with a strong mind and full faith of a more glorious state hereafter. Stature about six feet—weight 200. Death had no terror." Here was a man in the tradition of Vermonters.

Marlboro is notable today for its summer music festival featuring prominent artists. Here Captain Humphrey Hobbs and his company of forty were attacked by a very large Abnaki Indian party in 1748, led by Sackett. Both Hobbs and Sackett were famous as frontier fighters. In the four-hour battle the Indians lost many warriors, while only three of Hobbs' party were killed.

Many people will travel for miles to enjoy one of Vermont's famous game suppers. Among the best of these is the annual supper held each November in Dummerston. Here is Naulaka, the home designed by Rudyard Kipling for his use.

At Putney, John Humphrey Noyes began the sect that gained him considerable notoriety. He believed in the sharing of property, including the sharing of husbands and wives in what he called "complex marriage." Noyes was arrested and fled to New York. Today, Putney is headquarters for a very different group known as the Experiment for International Living.

The Scott Bridge at Townshend, 275 feet (84 meters) long, is the longest single-span covered bridge in Vermont. It is the first covered bridge selected for preservation by the Vermont Board of Historic Sites.

In the Cumberland County Courthouse at Westminster the state of New York once administered its interests in colonial Vermont.

Bellows Falls is the location of Steamtown Museum. Its collection of old-time steam trains and cars includes the diner-lounge from President Franklin D. Roosevelt's private train. Many of the old locomotives are in operating condition, and visitors may take a twenty-mile (thirty-two kilometer) ride behind one of them. The first person to survive a trip over Bellows Falls was an Abnaki woman. When she saw that she was caught in the current, she drank the whiskey she was taking to her husband and stretched out along the bottom of the canoe. She was fished out below the falls, safe but quite drunk.

When the Reverend John Williams was captured by the Indians in 1704 near present-day Rockingham, he preached to his fellow captives the first Protestant sermon given in Vermont.

Weston was once abandoned, but now it has many attractions for summer and fall visitors, including an attractive country store. The Weston Playhouse is one of the most beautiful small theaters in America. Summer musical programs are presented there as well as plays. The Vermont Guild of Old Time Crafts is located in Weston. A fine school of arts and crafts operates on the old Proctor farm near Cavendish.

Often called the Birthplace of Vermont, the Old Constitution House at Windsor has been preserved and restored as a historic shrine and museum. The first Vermont constitution was signed here in 1777.

One of the outstanding natural spectacles of Vermont is Quechee Gorge near Taftsville, a 1-mile-long (1.6 kilometers) chasm cut by the Ottaquechee River. Neighboring Woodstock holds a notable place in the history of sport. In January 1934, on a hill on Clinton Gilbert's farm, a continuous rope powered by a Model-T Ford engine hauled skiers uphill. This was the first ski tow in the United

*Though it was once abandoned, the town of Weston (above)
now has many attractions for summer and fall visitors.*

States and launched "a new era in winter sports." Woodstock claims to be the only town in which there are four church bells cast by Paul Revere.

In a national dedication ceremony in 1957 at Plymouth Notch, John Coolidge presented to the state a simple story-and-a-half white house, the boyhood home of his father, Calvin Coolidge. This is proving to be Vermont's most popular historic shrine, in a village which has been called the "most unchanged mountain hamlet in the state." The public may walk through the Coolidge barn and through

85

the house, looking into each of the rooms, all furnished just the way they were on the night Coolidge took his presidential oath of office there. The Wilder Barn in Plymouth features a display of early farming tools, implements, and related farm items.

The first alpine-type ski lift in the country was built on Pico Peak near Sherburne. Long Trail Lodge near Sherburne is known for the brook that wanders through its main lounge and the living trees that pierce its roof.

Between Sharon and Royalton is a striking monument to a man who may have the most enduring and far-reaching influence of all Vermonters—Joseph Smith. The Mormon religion, which he founded, has now taken root in almost all parts of the world, and has had a striking growth. The monument is said to be the largest single shaft of finished granite ever turned; it is 38 feet (11.6 meters) high and weighs 30 tons (27 metric tons). An inscription reads "Sacred to the Memory of Joseph Smith, The Prophet, Born here 23 December, 1805; Martyred, Carthage, Illinois, 27th June, 1844."

Skiing at Killington, one of the many Vermont ski areas.

Another nearby memorial is that of Justin Smith Morrill. His life-long residence at Strafford is now registered as a National Historic Landmark.

Rutland, the second largest city in Vermont, contains the world's deepest marble quarry, and there is a fine marble exhibit at nearby Proctor. The beautiful Church of Christ the King at Rutland makes especially effective use of native Vermont marbles. In the all-day celebration at Rutland of Vermont's admission to the union in 1791 a memorable toast was drunk: "The Union of Vermont with the United States: May it flourish like our pines and continue as unshaken as our mountains."

When Clarendon Springs became popular as a resort, it was one of the first mineral spas in the country. To encourage people to come and try the mineral waters, advertisers pointed out that the birthrate in the Clarendon area was unusually high.

The True Temper Tool Company at Wallingford is said to be the world's largest garden tool company. Natural attractions near Wallingford are the ice caves, where ice is found throughout the year. Even the boulders at the entrance are cold.

For more than a century Manchester has been one of Vermont's best-loved summer resorts, where members of the *Social Register* congregate. Robert Todd Lincoln, son of the president, had an estate at Manchester and died there in 1926. The nearness of the marble quarries is demonstrated by Manchester's marble sidewalks. The Southern Vermont Art Center houses exhibits of painting, photography, and sculpture.

Manchester was the site of the notorious Boorn murder trial. The Boorn brothers were sentenced to die after confessing to a murder. There was much embarrassment when the murdered man turned up very much alive, fortunately before the executions had taken place.

One of the country's famous war memorials is the 306-foot (93-meter) Bennington Battle Monument, once the world's highest. In 1964, the Vermont Board of Historic Sites commissioned Paul V. Winters to create a diorama of the second engagement action of the Battle of Bennington, and this now gives the visitor a telling view of the region's historic past.

Church in historic Bennington.

In the graveyard of the First Congregational Church rest many of the founders of Vermont, as well as five governors of the state.

Bennington Historical Museum and Art Gallery offers some especially interesting items of Vermont history, including the oldest known Stars and Stripes, and very valuable exhibits of prized antique Bennington pottery. On the grounds of the Soldiers' Home is a water jet said to be the world's highest natural fountain.

Where once stood the historic old Catamount Tavern at Bennington, where Ethan Allen and his Green Mountain Boys plotted against the New Yorkers and later against the British, there now stands a life-sized bronze statue of a mountain lion (catamount). This is a reminder of the stuffed one which once snarled his defiance at the enemies from above the door of the tavern. It is hard to tell whether the present catamount is really snarling. He may only be smiling as he reviews the success of his masters' descendants or, perhaps, even grinning a welcome to those who have come to pay tribute to the stirring and historic past.

Handy Reference Section

Instant Facts

Became the 14th state, March 4, 1971
Capital—Montpelier, settled 1787
Nickname—Green Mountain State
State motto—"Freedom and Unity"
State animal—Morgan horse
State bird—Hermit thrush
State tree—Sugar maple
State flower—Red clover
State insect—Honeybee
State song—"Hail, Vermont!"
Area—9,609 square miles (24,887 square kilometers)
Rank in area—43
Greatest length (north to south)—155 miles (249 kilometers)
Greatest width (east to west)—90 miles (145 kilometers)
Geographic center—3 miles (4.8 kilometers) east of Roxbury
Highest point—4,393 feet (1,339 meters), Mt. Mansfield
Lowest point—95 feet (29 meters), Lake Champlain
Mean elevation—1,000 feet (305 meters)
Number of counties—14
Population—504,000 (1980 projection)
Rank in population—48
Population density—52.4 per square mile (20.3 per square kilometer), 1980
            projection
Rank in density—30
Population center—In Granville, Addison County, 18 miles (29 kilometers)
            northwest of Middlebury
Illiteracy—0.6 percent
Birthrate—14.6 per 1,000
Infant mortality rate—15.3 per 1,000
Physicians per 100,000—186

Principal cities		
Burlington	38,633	(1970 census)
Rutland	19,293	
Bennington	14,586	
Brattleboro	12,239	
Essex	10,591	

You Have a Date with History

1609—Samuel Champlain is first European known to have visited area
1666—French build fort and shrine to Saint Anne on Isle La Motte
1690—English build fort at Chimney Point
1724—Fort Dummer begun, first permanent settlement
1741—King gives Vermont region to New Hampshire
1749—Bennington granted by Governor Wentworth of New Hampshire
1754—Captive Johnson born at Reading following Indian raid
1759—Rogers' Rangers destroy St. Francis Indian village
1763—Treaty of Paris confirms English control of area
1764—King George III proclaims Connecticut River as boundary of New York
1768—New York establishes Cumberland County
1769—First act of "revolt" against New York, at Bennington
1770—Green Mountain Boys organized
1777—Vermont becomes independent republic; battles of Hubbardton and
         Bennington
1780—Royalton Indian raid
1789—Death of Ethan Allen at Burlington
1790—New York claims settled for $30,000
1791—Statehood
1805—Montpelier named state capital
1813—U.S. fleet built at Vergennes
1816—Worst winter of Vermont history
1830—Chester A. Arthur born, Fairfield
1837—Thomas Davenport of Brandon invents electric motor
1859—Capitol building dedicated
1861—Civil War begins, in which 34,328 from Vermont serve
1864—Confederate raid on St. Albans
1866—Fenian raids
1872—Calvin Coolidge born at Plymouth
1881—Chester A. Arthur becomes president
1896—Vermont pioneers absentee voting
1910—Long Trail is begun
1917—America enters World War I, in which 16,000 from Vermont serve
1923—Calvin Coolidge inaugurated at Plymouth Notch
1927—Worst flood of Vermont history
1929—Lake Champlain bridge at Chimney Point opened
1941—Vermont "declares war" before the United States does
1943—Chaplain George Lansing Fox lost with the *Dorchester*
1957—Moore Dam completed
1964—Vermont reelects Democratic Governor Philip H. Hoff
1970—Land Use and Development Control Law passed
1973—Devastating Floods
1977—Republicans recapture governor's chair and Senate seat

Governors of Vermont

Thomas Chittenden 1778-1789
Moses Robinson 1789-1790
Thomas Chittenden 1790-1797
Paul Brigham 1797
Isaac Tichenor 1797-1807
Israel Smith 1807-1808
Isaac Tichenor 1808-1809
Jonas Galusha 1809-1813
Martin Chittenden 1813-1815
Jonas Galusha 1815-1820
Richard Skinner 1820-1823
C.P. Van Ness 1823-1826
Ezra Butler 1826-1828
Samuel C. Crafts 1828-1831
William A. Palmer 1831-1835
Silas H. Jennison 1835-1841
Charles Paine 1841-1843
John Mattocks 1843-1844
William Slade 1844-1846
Horace Eaton 1846-1848
Carlos Coolidge 1848-1850
Chas. K. Williams 1850-1852
Erastus Fairbanks 1852-1853
John S. Robinson 1853-1854
Stephen Royce 1854-1856
Ryland Fletcher 1856-1858
Hiland Hall 1858-1860
Erastus Fairbanks 1860-1861
Frederick Holbrook 1861-1863
J. Gregory Smith 1863-1865
Paul Dillingham 1865-1867
John B. Page 1867-1869
Peter T. Washburn 1869-1870
George W. Hendee 1870
John W. Stewart 1870-1872
Julius Converse 1872-1874
Asahel Peck 1874-1876
Horace Fairbanks 1876-1878
Redfield Proctor 1878-1880

Roswell Farnham 1880-1882
John L. Barstow 1882-1884
Samuel E. Pingree 1884-1886
Ebenezer J. Ormsbee 1886-1888
Wm. P. Dillingham 1888-1890
Carroll S. Page 1890-1892
Levi K. Fuller 1892-1894
Urban A. Woodbury 1894-1896
Josiah Grout 1896-1898
Edward C. Smith 1898-1900
Wm. W. Stickney 1900-1902
John G. McCullough 1902-1904
Charles J. Bell 1904-1906
Fletcher D. Proctor 1906-1908
George H. Prouty 1908-1910
John A. Mead 1910-1912
Allen M. Fletcher 1912-1915
Charles W. Gates 1915-1917
Horace F. Graham 1917-1919
Percival W. Clement 1919-1921
James Hartness 1921-1923
Redfield Proctor 1923-1925
Franklin S. Billings 1925-1927
John E. Weeks 1927-1931
Stanley C. Wilson 1931-1935
Charles M. Smith 1935-1937
George D. Aiken 1937-1941
William H. Wills 1941-1945
Mortimer R. Proctor 1945-1947
Ernest W. Gibson 1947-1950
Harold J. Arthur 1950-1951
Lee E. Emerson 1951-1955
Joseph B. Johnson 1955-1959
Robert T. Stafford 1959-1961
F. Ray Keyser, Jr. 1961-1963
Philip H. Hoff 1963-1969
Deane C. Davis 1969-1973
Thomas P. Salmon 1973-1977
Richard A. Snelling 1977-

Index

93

94

PICTURE CREDITS

ABOUT THE AUTHOR

With the publication of his first book for school use when he was twenty, **Allan Carpenter** began a career as an author that has spanned more than 135 books. After teaching in the public schools of Des Moines, Mr. Carpenter began his career as an educational publisher at the age of twenty-one when he founded the magazine *Teachers Digest.* In the field of educational periodicals, he was responsible for many innovations. During his many years in publishing, he has perfected a highly organized approach to handling large volumes of factual material: after extensive traveling and having collected all possible materials, he systematically reviews and organizes everything. From his apartment high in Chicago's John Hancock Building, Allan recalls, "My collection and assimilation of materials on the states and countries began before the publication of my first book." Allan is the founder of Carpenter Publishing House and of Infordata International, Inc., publishers of *Issues in Education* and *Index to U. S. Government Periodicals.* When he is not writing or traveling, his principal avocation is music. He has been the principal bassist of many symphonies, and he managed the country's leading non-professional symphony for twenty-five years.